HANDBOOK OF AUGMENTED REALITY TRAINING DESIGN PRINCIPLES

The *Handbook of Augmented Reality Training Design Principles* is for anyone interested in using augmented reality and other forms of simulation to design better training. It includes eleven design principles aimed at training recognition skills for combat medics, emergency department physicians, military helicopter pilots, and others who must rapidly assess a situation to determine actions. Chapters on engagement, creating scenario-based training, fidelity and realism, building mental models, and scaffolding and reflection use real-world examples and theoretical links to present approaches for incorporating augmented reality training in effective ways. The Learn, Experience, Reflect framework is offered as a guide to applying these principles to training design. This handbook is a useful resource for innovative design training that leverages the strengths of augmented reality to create an engaging and productive learning experience.

LAURA G. MILITELLO is a cofounder of Unveil, LLC, a start-up company that delivers augmented reality-based recognition skills training to combat medics, emergency responders, and others. She coauthored *Perspectives on Cognitive Task Analysis*, and she cohosts the Naturalistic Decision Making podcast. Her work supports people who make tough decisions in challenging situations.

CHRISTEN E. SUSHEREBA is a research associate at Unveil, LLC. She received her M.S. in Human Factors and Industrial/Organizational Psychology from Wright State University in Dayton, Ohio, USA, in 2018. She has spent the first decade of her career applying cognitive engineering and human factors methods to a variety of domains including military pararescue, emergency medicine, aviation, and human-automation teaming.

SOWMYA RAMACHANDRAN is a senior research engineer at Stottler Henke Associates. She has more than two decades of experience in designing rich, interactive, personalized learning experiences for professional training, and is excited about the use of artificial intelligence to enhance training and education. She holds a Ph.D. in Computer Science from The University of Texas at Austin, USA.

T0371538

HANDBOOK OF AUGMENTED REALITY TRAINING DESIGN PRINCIPLES

LAURA G. MILITELLO
Unveil, LLC

CHRISTEN E. SUSHEREBA
Unveil, LLC

SOWMYA RAMACHANDRAN
Stottler Henke Associates, Inc.

CAMBRIDGE
UNIVERSITY PRESS

Shaftesbury Road, Cambridge CB2 8EA, United Kingdom

One Liberty Plaza, 20th Floor, New York, NY 10006, USA

477 Williamstown Road, Port Melbourne, VIC 3207, Australia

314–321, 3rd Floor, Plot 3, Splendor Forum, Jasola District Centre, New Delhi – 110025, India

103 Penang Road, #05–06/07, Visioncrest Commercial, Singapore 238467

Cambridge University Press is part of Cambridge University Press & Assessment, a department of the University of Cambridge.

We share the University's mission to contribute to society through the pursuit of education, learning and research at the highest international levels of excellence.

www.cambridge.org
Information on this title: www.cambridge.org/9781009216173

DOI: 10.1017/9781009216166

First published 2023

A catalogue record for this publication is available from the British Library.

A Cataloging-in-Publication data record for this book is available from the Library of Congress.

ISBN 978-1-009-21617-3 Hardback
ISBN 978-1-009-21615-9 Paperback

We dedicate this book to the many practitioners who have allowed us to interview and observe them so we could learn about their work.

Laura G. Militello dedicates this book to her mom who loved books, and to Mark who puts up with her when she is in the throes of writing.

Christen E. Sushereba dedicates this book to her family, who have supported her unconditionally.

Sowmya Ramachandran dedicates this book to her parents who sacrificed much to get her to where she is today.

Contents

Figures

Tables

Preface

If you have picked up this book, chances are you are interested in the potential of augmented reality to improve training effectiveness and are looking for guidance. We found ourselves in the same situation as we began to explore the use of augmented reality for training combat medics. Combat medics must learn to quickly assess a patient and decide what actions to take, often in austere environments where security is a concern and resources are limited. The skills of the combat medic can mean the difference between life and death for their patients. We were captured by the idea that we could use augmented reality to help combat medics be even better prepared to save lives. Augmented reality technology makes it possible to project a virtual patient onto the physical world, opening up all sorts of possibilities for training to prepare medics to manage the tough situations they will face.

With the world of possibilities in front of us, but very little design guidance available, we worked with experienced instructors and pulled from our own experiences studying decision-making under stress and developing training. We learned a lot about augmented reality and our first training products were well received. Then, we received funding from the Defense Health Agency to both develop augmented reality training for combat medics *and* develop a set of evidence-based guidelines. Our project sponsor, Dr. Ray Perez, was tired of seeing flashy augmented reality applications that had limited training value. He asked us to review the scientific literature and draw lessons learned from existing training to identify design principles for developing effective augmented reality-based training, and so the seeds of this handbook were sown.

We wrote this handbook because we believe there is a growing community of trainers who are looking for design principles to guide their work as they incorporate augmented reality and related technologies into training. Many have failed to find training improvements after adding augmented or virtual reality training elements. We believe this is due to a lack of principled design, rather than the lack of potential for these technologies to improve training. There is nothing wrong with the technologies – the problem is with how the technologies are incorporated into training.

We have spent several years incorporating augmented reality into training for combat medics. Many of the examples in this handbook draw from this experience. However, the design principles are relevant to other domains, particularly jobs that require recognition skills or the ability to quickly size up a situation and know what to do. We hope these principles serve as a springboard for designers to creatively apply them to new training objectives.

We adopted a multidisciplinary and varied approach to developing the design principles outlined in this handbook. Being researchers, we looked for empirical data published about augmented reality training (studies are few, and results are mixed). We consulted other design principles for learning and training, particularly Richard Mayer's *Multimedia Learning* (Cambridge University Press, 2005). His work served as an inspiration to us; however, the body of research that Mayer applied to develop and refine his principles does not yet exist for augmented reality. Our solution to an almost complete lack of guidance was to explore empirical findings that could be extrapolated to augmented reality. We combined these extrapolations with implications from relevant theory and our own experiences developing augmented reality training.

One note about terms: There are many descriptors that refer to the addition of virtual content in an interactive experience – augmented reality, mixed reality, extended reality, and virtual reality. These terms are often loosely defined, and the labels and definitions evolve with the technology. In this handbook, we use the term "augmented reality" to refer to a blended virtual and physical environment. The widely popular game "PokémonGo" was an early example of how projecting a virtual object into the real world can create a compelling experience. In this game, players can see and interact with the virtual Pokémon, and still see the actual sidewalk, shops, and people that surround them. This concept has been expanded and adapted for use in entertainment, marketing, and training. Amusement parks project virtual characters onto the physical world to delight children. Some furniture companies offer an app that allows you to use your mobile phone to place virtual furniture in your home to help you decide which items to purchase. We have found that the integration of virtual content into the physical environment creates powerful training. Augmented reality allows us to represent many of the challenges of the real world in ways that were simply not practical previously. The increased realism creates an engaging learning experience that has the potential to improve transfer to on-the-job performance.

Writing this handbook has been a multidisciplinary collaboration between three colleagues and friends.

Ms. Militello is a recognized leader in the Naturalistic Decision Making community. She helped establish the Naturalistic Decision Making Association and is cohost of the Naturalistic Decision Making podcast. She is the cofounder of two small businesses. Unveil, LLC develops and delivers augmented reality training to combat medics as well as civilian emergency medical services. Applied Decision Science, LLC is a research and development company that studies expertise in high-stakes environments. She coauthored (with Robert Hoffman) *Perspectives on Cognitive Task Analysis* (Taylor & Francis, 2009), a leading textbook on cognitive task analysis. She has been developing strategies to support people who make decisions under stress for over thirty years.

Ms. Sushereba has spent the last twelve years studying Naturalistic Decision Making, exploring how people such as combat medics, helicopter pilots, and anesthesiologists make decisions under stress. She was part of the design team for the Virtual Patient Immersive Trainer (VPIT^{TM}), one of the first augmented reality training technologies available to combat medics. She is a trained human factors psychologist with a passion for designing solutions to improve how experts perform their jobs in high-stress environments.

Dr. Ramachandran has deep experience with a broad range of simulation-based training approaches including cognitive intelligent tutoring systems. She has developed training in a range of domains including combat search and rescue, combat medicine, civilian emergency medical services, and US Armed Forces tactical decision-making. She is a leader in learner-centered training and has spent much of her career collaborating with experienced instructors to develop creative approaches to assess learner knowledge and adapt training to learners' needs. She is known for her work integrating artificial intelligence into training applications.

If you are a student, a training designer, a software designer or developer, or an instructor, we have designed this handbook for you. We hope you find it a useful and fertile starting point from which to launch your own creative solutions to implementing augmented reality training.

Acknowledgments

We are lucky to have friends and colleagues who supported us in creating this book. Our colleagues at Unveil, John Hendricks, Oliver Smith, and Steve Wolf, were a sounding board and reality check for us as we articulated design principles. John Hendricks is a brilliant "creative technologist," whose ability to embrace the potential of what augmented reality can achieve was the driving force behind many of the augmented reality design seeds offered in this handbook. He has donated his time to create the images in this handbook. Oliver Smith has many years of experience as a US Air Force pararescue jumper and combat rescue officer. He has trained many young combat medics and generously shared his experiences with us. Steve Wolf is a visionary with a strong track record in moving from good ideas to actual products that people use. He challenged us to transform our technical report into an accessible and useful handbook.

Many thanks to Dr. Emily Patterson for her help in designing studies to evaluate our principles. Dr. Patterson led a team at the Ohio State University that conducted a series of studies. Dr. Olivia Hernandez and Lauren Mansour conducted studies to help us better understand the strengths and limitations of some of our early training prototypes. T. J. Seelig shared his experiences as a combat medic to inform scoring used in the studies. Dr. Patterson's colleagues in the Ohio State University Wexner Medical Center Emergency Department, including Dr. David Bahner, Dr. Michael Barrie, and Dr. Christopher San Miguel, helped shape our thinking as we generated early training prototypes for evaluation.

Our sponsor Dr. Ray Perez from the Office of Naval Research challenged us to articulate design principles and highlighted the need for this handbook. An earlier version of these design principles was developed at Dr. Perez's direction as part of a Small Business Technology Transfer Research (STTR) contract. That initial work was supported by the US Army Medical Research and Materiel Command (USAMRMC) under contract no. W81XWH-18-C and W81XWH-18-C-0151. The views, opinions, and/or findings contained in this report are those of the authors and should not be construed as an official Department of the Army position, policy, or decision unless so designated by other documentation.

Dick Stottler of Stottler Henke Associates, Inc., provided support for Dr. Ramachandran's writing, and his company provided many of the examples of successful training programs described in this handbook. We would like to acknowledge the contributions of the many research scientists and engineers at Stottler Henke to the development of these training systems.

Ben Beecroft, Sarah Beecroft, Jim Bliss, Ellen Deutsch, Reza Jalaiean, Fran Jerisk, Rachel Kennedy, Mary Jo McCarty, Mark Sisson, Oliver Smith, Eli Wagner, Michelle Wang, and Steve Wolf reviewed early versions or portions of this handbook and provided valuable feedback and suggestions for improving it.

Lastly, we would like to thank the many combat medics, helicopter pilots, physicians, nurses, military commanders, and others who have allowed us to observe them at work, interview them, and sit in on training over the years. The passion these experts bring to their work is inspiring. This handbook would never have come to be if they did not generously welcome us into their worlds.

CHAPTER I

Introduction

Our friend Oliver spent fifteen years as a pararescue jumper with the United States Air Force. A big part of this job is being ready to do whatever it takes to rescue people who have been injured, often in remote and sometimes hostile settings. He has jumped out of airplanes, fast-roped out of helicopters, performed open ocean rescues, and assembled mechanical advantage pulley systems to rescue injured people from the side of mountains. He has applied tourniquets to hemorrhage injuries; made incisions in patients' airways to enable breathing (called a cricothyroidotomy); performed other surgical procedures; and administered antibiotics and pain medications. Pararescue jumpers routinely locate and treat severely injured military personnel using only the equipment they carry on their backs, and arrange for safe transport to a higher level of care, often in hostile territory.

Mary is a highly experienced emergency department pediatrician who works at a major academic medical center that treats children from a large geographical region. Some children come straight to the emergency room from home; others are transported via helicopter, or transferred from a rural hospital that does not have the medical equipment or specialists needed to care for this particular child. Mary assesses and treats children with a broad range of injuries and illnesses; coordinates with nurses, respiratory therapists, subspecialists, and other members of the health-care team; and counsels, educates, and comforts parents – all in a noisy and sometimes chaotic setting with many distractions and stressors.

Oliver and Mary work under widely different conditions but they have several things in common. Both work under tremendous pressure and their patients' lives hang in balance based on their ability to perform skillfully. Another important thing they have in common is that, in addition to their responsibilities as highly skilled practitioners, they have the responsibility to train others. Oliver works with other senior personnel in his unit to develop creative ways to effectively train new pararescue jumpers, and to maintain the skills of even the most senior pararescue jumpers.

The pararescue community trains people in skills as diverse as creating mechanical advantage pulley systems and to safely scuba dive. Trainees learn the physical skills to jump from airplanes, run and swim long distances, and fast rope from helicopters in the dark. They also acquire the medical knowledge needed to treat patients. After completing this foundational training, they are assigned to a unit where senior personnel like Oliver help them integrate these skills, so they are truly prepared to provide medical care in some of the worst situations. Oliver and his colleagues design training exercises that include physical challenges, simulated enemy forces, and sophisticated medical manikins to hone the medical, physical, and stress management skills required to rescue and treat injured personnel in combat settings.

Mary, in addition to assessing and treating the children who come to the emergency room, is continually training and mentoring resident physicians. The residents have completed rigorous training in medical school and are now learning on the job to apply, extend, and adapt that learning to meet the challenges of a busy emergency department. Mary is always alert for gaps in their knowledge and looking for ways to help these physicians-in-training obtain the skills they will need to care for infants, teenagers, and everyone in between with a broad range of injuries and illnesses. In addition to routine, on-the-job training and mentoring, Mary runs a simulation center where senior faculty work with training designers to simulate important challenges physicians will face so they can practice assessing actors playing the role of patients and performing procedures on manikins. Mary is always seeking effective ways to provide physicians a realistic and safe environment to practice and refine their skills.

These are just two examples of the types of people we work with who are interested in exploring the strengths of augmented reality for creating effective training to help learners be better at very quickly sizing up a situation and acting. Both have the need to be able to create a broad range of training scenarios. They want to be able to depict virtual patients with many different injuries and simulate environmental factors such as the view from a helicopter or the sounds of a busy emergency room. In addition to virtual assets, they want trainees to use real-world equipment so they can "practice the way they fight" as military trainers frequently say. They also want principles to help them design effective training. Oliver, Mary, and other people like them who design training for people in high-stakes environments were the inspiration for this book.

Training to support people who routinely make decisions under stress often takes the form of elaborate and creative exercises. Firefighters use training grounds in which actual structure fires are created; US Navy personnel participate in exercises in which compartments fill with water and catch fire as they would in a sinking ship; in medical training, anesthetized live animals may be used to practice surgery and other interventions that are difficult to simulate. These immersive and realistic training experiences are considered critical to preparing people to make decisions under stress, to recognize what is going on and determine how to act. However, there are disadvantages to such approaches. This type of training is expensive, can at times endanger trainees, and often takes place in situations that make it difficult for instructors to provide timely feedback.

Augmented reality may provide some of the benefits of these carefully orchestrated and often large-scale training exercises without some of the drawbacks by presenting virtual objects in a physical environment (Sushereba et al., 2021; Zhu et al., 2014). Modern augmented reality technologies are more affordable, portable, and flexible than ever before. They are a powerful tool for presenting photorealistic images via handheld tablets and head-worn goggles. The popular Pokémon Go augmented reality game is a well-known example. Players look through the Pokémon app on their phone to see virtual Pokémon superimposed on the real world. Players "catch" Pokémon by throwing a virtual Poké ball at the Pokémon. They can see and interact with the virtual Pokémon, and also see the physical world around them. In a similar fashion, virtual objects such as patients, medical equipment, colleagues, and terrain features can be projected onto any surface, transforming a conference room or exam room into a simulation center. Figure 1.1 shows a learner wearing the HoloLens headset and viewing a virtual patient.

Augmented reality can be integrated into existing simulation centers. A virtual patient can be projected onto a physical manikin to show dynamic changes in the look of the patient while still providing an opportunity to practice medical interventions on the physical manikin. For example, Figure 1.2 depicts a virtual patient with a burn injury. Examining the panels from left to right, note how the patient's face swells and his eyes close as the injury progresses. In this case, the patient has inhaled superheated air, which can happen when fires break out in small spaces. The facial swelling, burns around the mouth, and singed nose hairs should prompt the learner to examine the airway for swelling and act quickly before the airway is completely obstructed. When experiencing the augmented reality training, the virtual patient's appearance is dynamic, allowing the learner to assess changes to the virtual patient's skin, rate of swelling, breathing, and facial expression over time.

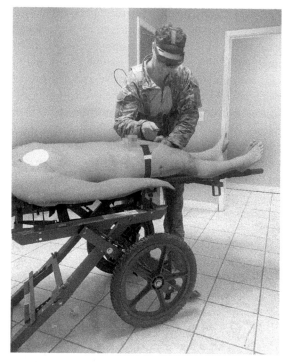

Figure 1.1 Example of a learner viewing a virtual patient through the HoloLens
headset

(a)   (b)   (c)

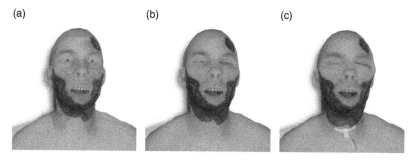

Figure 1.2 Example of a virtual patient with a burn injury developing over time

Augmented reality also enables interesting possibilities in terms of visually
highlighting specific cues in the virtual patient (or other virtual objects) to
guide the learner's attention or introduce an avatar in the form of

a colleague or supervisor who encourages learners to articulate their understanding of the situation and intended actions. There are many possibilities for leveraging augmented reality in training design, but few resources available to guide those designing augmented reality-based training.

This handbook is intended to support training technology developers, designers, and instructors in developing augmented reality training programs. We focus on training recognition skills because these skills form the foundation of the expertise needed to handle the complex situations that practitioners like Oliver and Mary face. By recognition skills we mean *the ability to rapidly size up a situation and know what actions to take.*

We draw on several related lines of research, including our own work focused on supporting combat medics and medical students in rapidly assessing a situation and knowing what to do. We include examples from studies of decision-making under pressure in diverse domains such as firefighting, piloting, and health care. Our intent in this book is to pull together theory, empirical research, and lessons learned to guide training developers in adapting existing (and developing new) training techniques that exploit the strengths of increasingly sophisticated augmented reality technologies.

To develop the eleven design principles presented in this handbook, we began by reflecting on what we believe to be important components of recognition skills training based on our experience studying decision-making in complex settings over the last thirty years. We then conducted an extensive literature search, looking for evidence to support or refute our hypothesized principles, as well as candidate principles we had not considered. We presented our draft principles at scholarly meetings to obtain input from training developers and researchers. Because much of our experience in designing and developing training using augmented reality has been in the context of military and civilian medicine, we obtained input from military medic instructors and emergency medicine faculty, leveraging their pragmatic, first-hand experiences. Although many of our examples draw from our experiences with combat medics and emergency medicine physicians, our intent is to articulate principles that are relevant to training recognition skills in a broad range of high-stakes domains including aviation, military command and control, surgery, elite sports, and others. Before describing the principles, we lay the groundwork with a discussion of recognition skills training and the theory that informs our approach.

1.1   Eleven Design Principles and the Organization of this Handbook

We offer eleven principles to guide the design of augmented reality-based recognition skills training. These principles are by no means exhaustive, but are ones that have empirical and theoretical support, and that we have found useful in designing augmented reality-based training. We group the principles into five categories: engagement, fidelity and realism, scenario building, supporting mental model construction, and scaffolding and reflection (Figure 1.3). These categories provide the organizing structure for this handbook. For each principle, we include a definition of the principle as well as a discussion of its importance for recognition skills, examples and empirical support, links to macrocognition theory, and a summary discussion. Here we provide a high-level introduction of each category that we will expand upon in the succeeding chapters.

We begin the discussion of design principles with a section on Engagement because it is foundational to the learning process and frequently touted as one of the strengths of augmented reality. This section offers principles to leverage the strengths of augmented reality to create a compelling training experience. The Scenario Building section emphasizes the value of training scenarios as fertile ground for a range of learning objectives, and for presenting cues in context to support transfer of recognition skills beyond training and onto the job. This section highlights the importance of including important cues that learners will need to look for and recognize in the real world, and including unexpected elements in scenarios to support adaptive skill development. The Fidelity and Realism

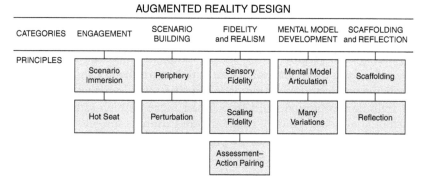

Figure 1.3 Eleven design principles organized into five categories

section explores trade-offs in determining which types of fidelity are critical to achieving specific learning objectives, emphasizing sensory, scaling, and functional fidelity for recognition skills training. The section on Mental Model Construction includes principles to aid learners in building and refining the internal representations of concepts, functions, and procedures they will need to manage the complexities they will face on the job. The Scaffolding and Reflection section explores strategies for tailoring training to the skill level of the learner, and for encouraging learners to reflect on and draw insights from the training experience.

Before delving into the design principles, we provide theoretical background relating to recognition skills training in Chapter 2. Chapters 3 through 7 detail the eleven design principles into five categories. Chapter 8 is a synthesis chapter, sharing how we use the Learn, Experience, Reflect framework to guide application of the design principles. We conclude with a concise summary of the design principles and a discussion of boundary conditions, contributions, and challenges for augmented reality in Chapter 9.

CHAPTER 2

Recognition Skills

2.1 Recognition Skills Training

Recognition skill is the ability to rapidly size up a situation and know what to do. When you are driving and see debris on the road, you may slow down, check your mirrors, and change lanes to avoid it. You can do this seemingly without thinking because you are an experienced driver and have developed recognition skills. When a paramedic comes to a scene, sees a patient hemorrhaging, and rapidly applies a tourniquet, they are using recognition skills.

Recognition skills are generally obtained and refined on the job, via experience. These skills are notoriously difficult to address in traditional training contexts, but for the domains in which they are critical – where there is time pressure, uncertainty, and often considerable risk – we see many examples of creative use of scenario-based training and apprenticeship/mentoring programs to support acquisition of recognition skills. Training designers in these domains are generally left to rely on a combination of ingenuity, trial and error, and adaptation of more general training principles to address training goals.

In this handbook, we propose a set of design principles specifically aimed at developing effective recognition skills training, with a focus on augmented reality applications. We leverage the training literature and our own experiences to articulate principles we have found to be particularly relevant to designing training for recognition skills. To be clear, many of these principles are based on learning theory (and related literatures) and are relevant for many types of training technologies. We focus on augmented reality because it is an emerging technology that paves the way to bring many of these theoretical principles to life in ways that were not practical previously.

Although we emphasize the value of recognition skills training, it is important to note that we do not expect novices to instantly become experts as a result of training. These skills take years to obtain in most contexts. Our intent is to design training that improves the learner's recognition skills for specific learning objectives, and also improves their *learning* skills. Effective training will help learners develop the skills they need to make the most of the experiences they encounter in training and in the real world. Recognition skills training is not about helping learners memorize facts and procedures; rather, our focus is on providing experiences that will help learners be better at using the information available to them to rapidly size up a situation and take appropriate actions.

2.2 Recognition Skills Theory

Our focus on recognition skills frames the design principles offered in this handbook. To set the stage, we share our perspective on recognition skills. There are many frameworks and taxonomies that are used to inform training design in general (e.g., Bloom et al., 1956; Norman, 2013). Although these taxonomies have been highly influential, we found them too general for our purposes. We are interested in developing training for people operating in dynamic, high-stakes environments. Our approach to training design extends naturally from the environments we train in; effective performance in high-stakes environments is typically driven by developing strong recognition skills.

Our theoretical approach to recognition skills is based on the recognition-primed decision model described by Klein and his colleagues (Klein et al., 1988). This model highlights that experienced people are often able to quickly recognize a situation as familiar, and based on that recognition, generate an effective course of action. In many cases, they are not even aware that they have made a decision. Daniel Kahneman describes this as "thinking fast" or "system 1 thinking" in his book, *Thinking Fast and Slow* (Kahneman, 2011). This model of decision-making is most thoroughly described in Gary Klein's book, *Sources of Power* (Klein, 1998). An illustrative example comes from a study of firefighters. One fireground commander described an incident in which he arrived on the scene of a fire and immediately recognized it as a kitchen fire in a single-family dwelling. He had seen this type of fire many times before and it was instantly recognizable. Based on his rapid assessment, he instructed his crew to enter through the front of the dwelling to knock down the seat of the fire in the kitchen. Because of this rapid reaction, they were able to save much of the structure. The fireground commander did not recall making a decision as he recounted the story. However, when probed further by the interviewer, he explained that he had seen other crews try to attack this type of fire from the back through windows, driving the fire further into the structure; he knew that was a poor course of action. He knew what to do without deliberation because he had seen similar fires many times, and observed which strategies were most effective (Klein et al., 1988; Klein et al., 2010).

In addition to the concept of quickly sizing up a situation and acting, another key component of recognition-primed decision-making is that decisions are not a single choice point. Rather, they are a process that includes assessing, acting, and reassessing. Often actions are taken with specific expectations about how the actions will influence the situation. Decision-makers continue to assess as the situation unfolds noting violated expectancies and surprising developments that refine their understanding of the situation. The decision-maker's assessment of the situation is in many ways a hypothesis that can be tested by taking actions and observing the results.

Recognition-primed decisions have been documented by skilled performers in many settings. A US Army Apache pilot described a situation in which he saw a small swirl of dust on the ground that was going against the current wind patterns in the desert. He quickly recognized this as an indicator that a huge sandstorm was about to roll in. He was able to rapidly divert and avoid getting caught in adverse weather conditions that would put his ability to safely fly the helicopter at risk (Militello et al., 2019). A neonatal intensive care nurse described a situation in which she conducted a routine assessment on a premature infant and knew immediately that the child was developing a potentially deadly infection in the bowel called "necrotizing enterocolitis." When asked to describe the infant, she recalled glassy eyes, pale skin, and a firm belly. She noted that the infant had not digested much of her most recent meal. These are all symptoms that are common in premature infants, but when observed in combination, the experienced nurse quickly recognized that this child was at risk (Militello & Lim, 1995).

These stories in which experienced personnel are able to quickly size up a situation and know what to do in spite of rapidly changing conditions, uncertainty, and distractions appear across many domains (Klein, 1998). The goal of recognition skills training is to help learners recognize critical cues and patterns so they can quickly intervene. We focus on three components of recognition skills: knowing what to attend to, creating meaning, and evaluating.

2.2.1 Knowing What to Attend To

Many researchers have come to the conclusion that experts are better at noticing relevant information than people with less experience (Gibson, 1969; Kellman, 2002; Kellman & Garrigan, 2009; Petrov et al., 2005; Shanteau, 1992). For some time, scientists thought that experts attended to more information than novices. However, Jim Shanteau and his colleagues at Kansas State University studied experienced and inexperienced accountants, physicians, nurses, and livestock judges only to discover that it is not the number of cues noticed that differentiates experts from others, rather, experts are better at determining which cues are important (Shanteau, 1992). Studies of medical radiologists (Hoffman et al., 1968), medical pathologists (Einhorn, 1974), stockbrokers (Slovic, 1969), and clinical psychologists (Goldberg, 1968) also found that skilled performers relied on a small number of particularly relevant cues.

Acquiring this skill of noticing relevant information is challenging because which cues are most important will vary depending on the situation. Less experienced people may be distracted by irrelevant information, slowing their reaction time. They may miss important cues, leading to incorrect assessments. They may find themselves anchoring on one piece of data and ignoring or explaining away contradictory information (Klein, et al., 2006a). Often, people learn to recognize critical cues by trial and error. When they make an incorrect assessment, they go back over the situation in their minds to determine what they missed. For example, in interviews with resident (trainee) emergency department pediatricians, resident physicians often recounted incidents in which other members of the health-care team recognized that a child was seriously ill before the resident did. The residents were able to describe the critical cues in retrospect, even if they did not notice them or understand their significance in the moment (Patterson et al., 2016).

2.2.2 Creating Meaning

Experts do not just know what to look for, they are also able to create meaning. An expert and a novice can look at the same situation and draw very different conclusions. Hoffman et al. (2010) emphasized that perception of cues is not sufficient for skilled performance; the cues must also be *meaningfully integrated*. As a result, expert recognition involves the ability to rapidly and effortlessly see meaningful information where others often cannot (Gibson, 2000; Goldstone & Barsalou, 1998). This is related to the concept of chunking, famously studied in the context of chess expertise. Researchers discovered that experienced chess players were able to extract meaning from brief exposure to chess boards depicting different configurations in ways that less experienced chess players could not (Chase & Simon, 1973b). Experts could view a midgame or endgame and remember it clearly, whereas novice chess players could not. However, when shown scrambled chess boards, the experts did no better than the novices at remembering the placement of chess pieces. For experts, the mid- and endgame configurations had meaning and were remembered as chunks rather than individual chess piece positions.

Patterson and her colleagues studied expert and novice differences in sepsis recognition by emergency department pediatricians (Patterson et al., 2016). Rapid recognition and intervention of sepsis is critical as delays in treatment often lead to significantly poorer outcomes and even death (Odetola et al., 2008). These investigators found that resident physicians (considered novices in this study) and experienced physicians recalled many of the same cues in recounting challenging incidents involving sepsis. The experienced physicians, however, also recalled the significance of the cues, the hypotheses they informed, and how others in the room often did not understand the significance of those cues initially. Experienced physicians used their understanding of the situation to form hypotheses about the patient's conditions. These hypotheses, in turn, informed which tests they ordered, what actions they took, and how they interpreted findings from tests and patient responses to interventions. The experienced physicians were able to create meaning from the cues available; the resident physicians noted many of the same cues but did not understand their significance, limiting their ability to develop plausible hypotheses that would drive their actions.

The data-frame model of sensemaking describes *how* people create meaning (Klein et al., 2006b). This model describes how an individual's prior experiences greatly influence what cues are considered relevant and how they are interpreted or meaningfully integrated. A person's cognitive "frame" drives what is considered relevant data, and what catches your attention. At the same time, the data in the environment influence what frame is invoked. As new information becomes available, the frame may be expanded, adapted, or discarded for one that better explains the situation. This implies that two experts may interpret the same situation differently, but both interpretations are likely to be reasonable and useful. Inexperienced people, however, may have difficulty creating meaning at all. An inexperienced clinician may carefully document a fever, lethargy, and elevated heart rate for a patient following surgery, but fail to put these individual cues together to consider that an infection or sepsis may be developing. These skills are typically acquired via experience on the job. Similarly, pharmacists sometimes notice drug–drug interactions that physicians miss. Both the pharmacist and the physician have access to information about the patient's symptoms and medication list. However, pharmacists tend to have a larger experience base of observing combinations of medications and side effects, allowing them to notice the right cues, see patterns, and make meaning that others cannot.

2.2.3 *Evaluating*

One key component of working effectively under time pressure is having strategies for quickly evaluating interventions *before* acting and continuing to monitor the situation for new information so that the plan can be revised as needed. The concept of mental simulation appears in many research traditions (Einhorn & Hogarth, 1981; Kahneman & Tversky, 1982; Klein & Crandall, 1995). It has been described as a way of starting with what is known and playing it forward to what might occur in the future, or playing it backward in time to imagine what may have occurred in the past to create the current situation. The recognition-primed decision model describes mental simulation as a streamlined strategy for imagining a potential course of action in one's head to identify flaws and refine the plan (Klein et al., 1988). The data-frame model of sensemaking describes how experienced practitioners update their understanding of the situation as new information becomes available (Klein et al., 2006b). Although evaluating one's understanding of the situation and planned actions is less prominent in the literature than knowing what to attend to and creating meaning, this skill is critical to noticing and recovering from errors and for avoiding fixation errors.

Our research team heard many examples of mental simulation during a project in which we interviewed US Army pilots. In Army aviation, mental simulation is used routinely in preparation for each mission. Referred to as mission rehearsal, team members meet to go over the plan and mentally walk through each component's role prior to a mission. Furthermore, individual pilots report that they continually mentally simulate as the mission unfolds, constantly comparing the current state of events to the plan, anticipating potential problems, and developing contingencies. For example, a helicopter pilot recounted an incident when he was serving as Air Mission Commander, supporting a team of Army Rangers on the ground:

> This pilot was responsible for managing a team of two Apache helicopters, four Black Hawk helicopters, and two drones. The Black Hawk helicopters would be used to carry a Ranger team including a dog and a translator to the area where they were needed, and the Apache helicopters and drones would be used to provide security. Timing was important because they were moving to an area of known hostile activity. This was a *hasty* mission, meaning there had not been days of planning; rather, a need had arisen and they were responding quickly to complete a time-sensitive mission. It was critical that they move as quickly as possible to give adversaries limited time to respond to the Rangers' presence. The Air Mission Commander recalled mentally simulating how they would manage a range of common problems if they were to arise. This included things such as reduced visibility due to dust and wind, as dust storms were an ever-present concern in this terrain. Another common risk for aging aircraft flying frequently in sandy, dusty conditions is delays due to maintenance issues. He was also aware that one aircraft had a faulty radio and was considering the implications and mentally simulating different workarounds. In addition to these common problems, on this particular mission, there were other elements that he needed to account for in his mental simulations. Specifically, they were transporting a dog and an interpreter with the Rangers. He knew that dogs required extra attention on helicopters because they get scared, so the dog would need to travel with his handler. He knew that the interpreter needed to travel with key members of the Ranger team. While they were still on the ground, before they had even picked up the Rangers, he was mentally simulating what would happen if one of the helicopters did not start up. How would he cross load the Rangers, the dog, the interpreter, and the personnel who were all key to the mission if they only had three Black Hawk helicopters rather than four as initially planned?

By mentally simulating a range of potential problems and evaluating various contingencies for managing them, Air Mission Commanders can anticipate and adapt to problems as they emerge, and sometimes prevent them altogether. To do this, the Air Mission Commander (or any operator) must have accurate and robust mental models (Rouse & Morris, 1986) that can serve as the basis for the mental simulation.

Our theoretical approach evolved as part of the Naturalistic Decision Making movement that emerged in the late 1980s. In addition to the recognition-primed decision model (Klein et al., 2010) and the data-frame model of sensemaking (Klein et al., 2006b), this community has conducted research that addresses many aspects of decision-making in complex environments including team coordination, managing uncertainty and risk, problem detection, establishing and maintaining common ground, managing attention, and planning (especially dynamic replanning as a situation unfolds). Given the breadth of cognitive processes explored by naturalistic decision-making researchers, many have begun to use the label "macrocognition" to describe this theoretical approach (Klein et al., 2000; Klein et al., 2003; Miller & Patterson, 2018; Patterson & Hoffman, 2012; Schraagen et al., 2008). In short, macrocognition is the study of cognitive processes used by people who make decisions in complex settings and includes processes such as sensemaking, managing uncertainty, detecting problems, managing attention, and coordinating (Klein et al., 2000). We adopt this same convention, using the term "macrocognition" throughout this handbook. For each principle in this handbook, we articulate important links to the macrocognition literature.

2.3 Scenario-Based Training

Our emphasis is on scenario-based training, so we consider each principle in this context. We use the term "scenario-based" to refer to training that places the learner in a situation they must assess and manage. The scenario may unfold over time, or could represent a snapshot in time. The scenario may be designed for individual learning experiences, or for team training. Scenario-based training encompasses a broad range of training media including text, live actors, augmented reality, and other simulation technologies, any of which can be used in combination with others. Scenarios are generally designed to address specific learning objectives. For the training we develop, learning objectives are generally associated with recognition skills, generally incorporating specific task components (e.g., distinguish hemorrhage injuries best treated with direct pressure from those requiring a tourniquet). We recommend learning needs assessment to articulate learning objectives, inform scenario design, support trade-off decisions regarding fidelity, and guide the design of scaffolding techniques. We find cognitive task analysis methods valuable for unpacking cognitive skills, critical cues, and complexities associated with recognition skills (Hoffman & Militello, 2008; Militello & Hutton, 1998).

With regard to content, each training scenario is designed to address specific learning objectives; often a series of scenarios will be combined into a learning module to support complex learning objectives. Scenario-based training can be instructor-led or self-guided. It can be relatively "tech-lite" using actors and simple tools, or it can be "tech-heavy" using advanced tools and automation. Stand-alone training (i.e., training with no instructor present) may be instantiated in an intelligent tutoring system that uses artificial intelligence to assess learner performance and provide customized support. The training session may include a didactic component to explain processes and concepts, as well as a debrief session to provide feedback and encourage reflection. Scaffolding and real-time feedback may be delivered by a live instructor, initiated by the learner, or introduced by artificial intelligence. The design principles discussed in this handbook are envisioned in the context of scenario-based training, emphasizing strategies for using augmented reality technologies to enhance the learning experience.

It is important to point out that although the focus of this book is on scenario-based augmented reality training design, creating compelling scenarios using augmented reality technology is an important part of training design but not the whole story. We use a Learn, Experience, Reflect framework to help us frame the entire training experience. The Learn component focuses on determining what declarative knowledge will be required for trainees to make the most of the training scenarios. The Experience component refers to the scenario-based experiential portion of the learning. The Reflect component refers to the training features that support the learner in reflecting on the experience, integrating knowledge, and discovering new insights. See Chapter 8 for more about the Learn, Experience, Reflect component.

2.4 Summary and Discussion

This handbook is intended to aid training designers as they create recognition skills training that leverages augmented reality technologies to implement training principles in new and creative ways. We have identified design principles that are particularly relevant to recognition skills training, drawing from the training and education literatures as well as our own work creating training for combat medics and medical students. The theoretical basis for our approach to recognition skills training is based primarily on the recognition-primed decision model (Klein et al., 2010). We articulate links to this model of decision-making, as well as other important research from the naturalistic decision making and macrocognition communities.

We emphasize three key components of recognition skills: knowing what to attend to, creating meaning, and evaluating. Our focus is primarily on training for dynamic, high-stakes domains characterized by uncertainty such as health care and military operations. The principles in this handbook are intended to create training that supports learners in building the foundation necessary for rapid recognition in these complex settings. Notably, acquiring recognition skills happens over time and with experience; thus, we aim to create training experiences that give learners the tools they will need to learn from and make the most of each training experience they encounter, whether in training or on the job.

CHAPTER 3

Engagement

The issue here is very simple. The more a learner is engaged by the material, the more powerful the training experience. Learners will pay closer attention, suffer less boredom, be less distracted, and quite likely will remember more material and apply what they have experienced. And augmented reality, because it immerses the learner in the material and the scenarios, is a powerful way to create engagement.

To effectively acquire new knowledge and skills from a training experience, learners must be engaged. This can be a challenge, particularly for those who work in high-risk jobs and have little patience for training that is perceived as an unwanted interruption of duties and does not seem relevant to the challenges they face. The visual fidelity (and perhaps the novelty) of augmented reality can be intrinsically engaging in the way that video games and amusement park rides are. However, once the "cool factor" wears off, the underlying design of training must remain relevant and keep learners actively engaged so they can reap the full benefits of the training. Aspects of engagement that go beyond novelty include a belief that the training content is directly applicable to the work, the feeling that the learner is in control, and a sense of immersion.

We include this section on engagement first in the discussion of design principles because it is foundational to the learning experience. The training design principles outlined in this handbook are intended to aid instructional designers in creatively harnessing the "cool factor" of augmented reality to apply evidence-based training principles. In this spirit, the Scenario Immersion Principle encourages the creation of a compelling and immersive learning experience. The Hot Seat Principle advocates for creating a training experience in which the learner feels a sense of responsibility and control for managing the situation. Scenario-based training makes it possible to safely place learners in situations in which they have little support or resources to fall back on, and therefore must determine how to manage the situation on their own. This may be particularly important for learners who are preparing for a role of increased responsibility such as medical students preparing to become resident physicians, or combat medics preparing for deployment.

3.1 Scenario Immersion Principle

Scenario Immersion Principle. Scenario-based training that creates a sense of the learner's presence in the scenario supports engagement.

3.1.1 *What Do We Mean by Immersion?*

Immersion refers to the sense of "being there" (Heeter, 1992; Psotka, 1995). The learner is able to focus on the training experience to the exclusion of the real world to some extent. The learner is not simply reading or hearing about the training scenario but feels a part of it. Consider a VR bone simulator developed by Greg Wiet and Don Stredny at the Ohio State University to train surgeons to place cochlear implants (Wiet et al., 2002; Wiet et al., 2012). The surgeon-in-training wears 3D glasses to view a 3D image of the skull on a computer screen. The learner holds a pen-like instrument that functions like a surgical drill. In addition to the visual feedback on the screen, the learner receives tactile and auditory feedback through the drill. In other words, learners see a 3D image of a skull, hold an instrument shaped like a drill, and actually feel the vibration and pressure of the drill against the bone as they create a space for the cochlear implant. This type of trainer is immersive in a way that simply cannot be attained with readings, lectures, and videos about cochlear implant surgery.

Immersion does not necessarily require that the training faithfully represents every aspect of the real world. Mechanisms that promote immersion have been described in different ways. Some describe different levels of immersion including engagement, engrossment, and total immersion (Brown & Cairns, 2004). Although initially used to describe immersion in the context of video games, these levels can easily be adapted to describe levels of immersion in training. The first level, engagement, suggests that learners must have interest, time, and find the technology usable enough to participate. The second level, engrossment, indicates that emotional attachment and focused attention contribute to a sense of immersion. The third level, total immersion, refers to the sensation that one is present in the blended physical and virtual training environment and is fully absorbed in the experience (Cheng et al., 2015).

We highlight two components of immersion in this discussion. First, engagement in the training experience is necessary for immersion to occur. When learners are emotionally and cognitively engaged, and feel a sense of control over the simulated world, they are better able to suspend disbelief, increasing the sensation that the virtual experience is real (Sherman & Craig, 2018). This sense of control and engagement allows learners to focus attention on interacting with the simulated environment, which creates a sense of presence within the training scenario (Waterworth et al., 2002; Zhang et al., 2017). Furthermore, when learners feel emotionally and cognitively engaged with a sense of control over the simulated world, they are more motivated to learn and explore within the simulated environment (Isen, 2000; Zajonc, 1980). They may be more willing to "buy in" and participate as if the activity were real even if some aspects of the simulation are not completely accurate. We find in our reading of the literature that sometimes engagement is described as a component of immersion and in other places immersion is characterized as a condition of engagement. Because engagement and immersion are so tightly linked, our discussion of immersion includes strategies for increasing engagement as well.

Second, we find the use of scenario-based training to be foundational to immersion, particularly for training in dynamic, high-stakes domains. The notion that new knowledge and skills are most effectively transferred when the learner is immersed in realistic scenarios and contexts is described as situated learning (Brown et al., 1989; Jean & Wenger, 1991). Situated learning is an extension of apprenticeship models of learning and emphasizes the use of stories and scenarios to "situate" learning in the social and physical world of work. As such, our discussion of immersion focuses largely on strategies for creating scenario-based training that present learners with realistic challenges in realistic contexts.

Augmented and virtual reality are sometimes described in general as immersive technologies; however, before taking the discussion of immersion further, it is useful to clarify terms. Augmented and virtual reality are often loosely defined and in fact have changed over time as technology has evolved. Early versions of augmented and virtual reality were computer-based; the learner was represented as an avatar and interacted with a virtual world via a standard computer keyboard and mouse, or specialized game controllers. This type of experience is still very common in both training and computer gaming applications, and many find themselves immersed in the experience. More recent technology moves the augmented reality experience into the physical world. The learner uses a phone, tablet, or wearable headset, through which virtual objects are projected onto the physical world, allowing the user to interact with the virtual objects while maintaining context in the physical world. The ability to interact with virtual and physical elements as you would in the real world can create a sense of immersion. Related terms include hybrid reality, mixed reality, and location-based augmented reality. Virtual reality is distinct from augmented reality in that it generally refers to technology that creates a virtual environment – the whole world the learner inhabits is computer generated. In some cases, virtual reality is implemented in a room-sized cave virtual environment – effectively blocking out the real world. In other cases, virtual reality is implemented via a portable head-worn device that does not require a dedicated facility. Yet another type of virtual reality is screen based. All three types of virtual reality attempt to immerse the learner in the computer-generated world, presenting visual, auditory, and sometimes tactile stimuli, increasing the sensation that the user is present in the training environment. The whole range of augmented and virtual technologies is sometimes referred to collectively as extended reality.

Augmented and virtual reality have powerful advantages in terms of immersion over other training modalities. Although scenario-based training is generally intended to be immersive by design, augmented reality amplifies the effect. Learners do not have to view the world through someone else's perspective as they do when viewing images or videos; rather they see objects from their own point of view. Furthermore, they can move around objects or get closer or further away, to view objects from different perspectives just as they would in the real world. One goal of scenario-based training that uses augmented and virtual reality is to create a sense that the learner is able to perceive and act as they would in the real world. This additional realism in the way one interacts with the virtual objects creates a sense of being in the simulation.

3.1.2   Why Is Immersion Important?

Research supports the notion that interactive lessons increase student engagement, (Bulger et al., 2008), and experienced trainers attest to this as well. In fact, the idea that people learn more deeply when they are actively engaged is a basic tenet of many learning theories (Grabinger, 1996; Mayer, 2003; Pearce et al., 2005). Immersion creates a type of active learning that fosters both emotional and cognitive engagement. In scenario-based training, the learner becomes a decision-maker in the scenario. The ability to interact with life-like patients, equipment, and colleagues can evoke emotions similar to those one is likely to experience on the job. Medics may feel a sense of urgency, compassion, and heightened awareness that comes with treating patients; military leaders may feel a sense of responsibility and focus that comes with tactical decision-making. In fact, experiencing these heightened emotions during training may better prepare learners to manage stress in the real world, sometimes referred to as stress inoculation training (Robson & Manacapilli, 2014). Dirkx (2001) characterizes the dynamic nature of emotion in training. In the course of a training experience, a learner may move from frustration to excitement or boredom to fascination. The use of emotionally charged images and scenarios can prepare learners to anticipate and manage emotions such as frustration or fear so that they are able to engage cognitively in spite of stressful conditions.

With regard to cognitive engagement, immersion in the scenario may go a long way toward evoking active sensemaking and problem-solving that is a goal of so many training programs. The sense of immersion may hold the learner's attention and spur the curiosity needed for cognitive engagement. Some suggest that cognitive engagement can lead to a state of absorption or flow, where the learner is so involved in the simulation that they are not only expending mental energy but also creating it; they are energized by the training (Csikszentmihalyi et al., 2014; Esteban-Millat et al., 2014; Ghani & Deshpande, 1994). Others have highlighted the complex interaction between emotional and cognitive engagement in learning, emphasizing that emotions influence perception, attention, memory, decision-making, sensemaking, and problem-solving (Dirkx, 2001; Pekrun, 2011; Picard et al., 2004). For the kinds of high-stakes domains that require recognition skills, immersive scenarios that create both emotional and cognitive engagement may have better transfer to the real-world stressors that learners will face on the job.

3.1.3 Examples and Empirical Support

The very nature of augmented reality training may support immersion; however, it is not clear how much of this can be attributed to its novelty. Most evaluations focus on prototype or new training interventions; much less data are available about learner experiences with immersion and engagement over time. Therefore, we recommend leveraging other supportive factors to amplify the immersive benefits native to augmented reality and increase the likelihood that the training will continue to be immersive and engaging when the novelty has worn off. We draw from reviews of related research to summarize and discuss factors that support immersion and motivation. (See Nash et al., 2000 and Halverson & Graham, 2019 for a more detailed discussion.)

Developing training that has personal relevance and meaning is believed to foster engagement in important ways (Wang & Kang, 2006). Some authors suggest that the learner's willingness to interact with virtual elements plays an important role in the experience of immersion (Witmer & Singer, 1994, 1998). Setting the stage so that the learner understands how the training content relates to the job, and the gaps in performance that occur when this type of skill is not mastered may motivate learners to actively engage and interact with the training environment, increasing the likelihood of an immersive experience. For example, in training designed to aid non-medical military personnel as they become proficient in applying tourniquets, training might begin with information about the life-saving ability of a simple tourniquet and data showing how many military personnel with hemorrhage injuries are saved because a tourniquet was applied correctly, and how many do not survive because a tourniquet was applied incorrectly.

Another factor believed to foster engagement is the inclusion of links to prior knowledge and skills (Merrill, 2002). This is most easily done in training that extends over time and builds, or in the context of refresher training. For example, the Trainer for Advanced Life Support in Austere Regions (TALSAR) is an augmented reality-based trainer designed to help combat medics prepare to treat non-routine patients (Militello et al., 2021). In this case, military-aged males with combat injuries are considered routine because these are the types of patients combat medics commonly treat. TALSAR encourages medics to build on the skills they already have by calling attention to important differences between routine and non-routine patients. For example, a training module on pediatric injuries highlights how assessing an infant for traumatic head injury is different from assessing an adult. The intent is to link the new skill (assessing an infant) to a skill experienced medics use routinely (assessing adults), so they can quickly determine what existing knowledge is still relevant and note important differences to consider when treating an infant. Learning strategies that activate existing knowledge and skills, and encourage learners to extend what they know and can do, are engaging and support immersion.

The nature of learning goals may also influence engagement and immersion. Highly influential research conducted by Dweck and Leggett (1988) emphasized the importance of learning-oriented goals over performance-oriented goals in supporting learner engagement and immersion. They found that students who focused on performance (i.e., getting the highest test scores, being fastest or strongest, winning awards) were more likely to get discouraged, become disengaged, and give up when faced with a challenging task. Students who focused on learning-oriented goals, in contrast, were more likely to persist, maintain engagement, and try different strategies in the face of a difficult task. This notion of learning goals is very well accepted in the error management training literature in which learners are encouraged to make mistakes during training, and reminded: "The more errors you make, the more you learn" (Keith & Frese, 2008, p. 60). Error management training that emphasizes the value of making mistakes and learning from them over perfect performance during training has been shown to improve retention over time and support skill transfer to novel but related conditions not presented in training. While Dweck and Leggett's initial research led many to emphasize learning goals over performance goals, some research suggests that a combination of performance and learning goals may be effective (Eppler & Harju, 1997).

Another factor that fosters engagement and immersion is a sense of mystery and surprise. Training scenarios should be authentic and challenging, and for high-stakes tasks this generally means there is uncertainty and the situation takes unexpected turns. Scenarios that create uncertainty by partially revealing knowledge are both realistic and engaging (Brown, 1997). This encourages the learner to actively problem solve as they generate hypotheses and search for information that confirms or disconfirms their understanding of the situation (Arnone, 2003). Many training approaches take this approach. ShadowBox^{TM} is a training approach that focuses on cognitive skills development (Klein & Borders, 2016). ShadowBox uses text-based scenarios that require the learner to commit to an action or set of priorities early in the scenario when there is much uncertainty, and offers opportunities to reassess actions and priorities as the situation unfolds and more information is available. Plot twists are introduced that offer an opportunity to reframe the situation entirely. A similar approach is used with the Stratagems trainer for combat search and rescue helicopter pilots (Newsome et al., 2020). Rather than using a text-based scenario, Stratagems uses a video game platform to place the learner in the first-person perspective. Scenarios are designed so that the learner must begin the mission without some key information due to time pressure. Because of the urgency of the mission, learners do not have time to assemble all the information they would like before taking off to perform the rescue. As the scenario unfolds, they are able to obtain key information via radio communications. Some scenarios include unexpected twists. For example, the initial report may have been that there were two injured personnel, but upon arrival the learner discovers that there are four, forcing the learner to reconsider how to load the aircraft so that it can safely take off and return in spite of high altitudes and heat.

Gorini and colleagues (2011) explored different strategies for creating engagement and immersion in scenario-based interactions. They conducted a study in which college students were presented a virtual hospital. Some were asked to find blood containers by exploring the many corridors and rooms in the virtual hospital. Others were asked to complete the same task but were asked to imagine that they were a doctor who had to find and bring a container with a rare type of blood back to the main hospital where a child was waiting for a life-saving transfusion and that there was a mad murderer wandering around the hospital trying to kill them to prevent them from saving the sick child. Those who were in the role of the doctor (i.e., the "hot seat") showed increased heart-rate variation between the baseline and the virtual exploration, and an even higher heart-rate activation when they encountered the mad murderer. They also reported a greater sense of presence in the scenario than those who were simply asked to find blood containers.

Incorporating personal relevance and meaning, links to prior knowledge and skills, an emphasis on learning-oriented goals, and a sense of mystery and surprise into augmented reality training can create a highly immersive and engaging learning experience. High-fidelity audio and visual elements that allow learners to interact with the blended physical–virtual world create a powerful sense of presence. Virtual equipment as well as virtual adversaries, patients, and team members can add to the realism of the experience. Equipment and supplies from the physical world can be used so that learners get experience manipulating the tools they will use on the job. For example, Figure 3.1 depicts a combat medic inserting an IV into a manikin with a virtual patient overlay using a needle from her medical kit. Virtual mentors and supervisors can be introduced to ask questions and prompt the learner to incorporate instruction and hints while maintaining immersion. Augmented reality technology allows developers to control the pace of the scenario to maximize immersion, relevance, and learning value. A condition or scenario that unfolds over long periods of time can be shortened to make links between actions and outcomes apparent – although without the right context this approach can lead learners to have unrealistic expectations. Conversely, situations that are highly dynamic and require rapid assessment and response can be presented at realistic time scales but paused to relieve time pressure and encourage the

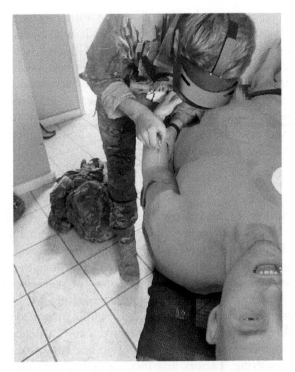

Figure 3.1 Combat medic inserts an IV into a manikin with a virtual patient overlay

learner to take a more effective path through the scenario. Augmented reality makes it easy to replay a scenario many times allowing the learner to practice until mastery is achieved.

3.1.4 Links to Macrocognition

Recognition skills are generally believed to be based on experiences and are typically acquired on the job (Klein et al., 1988). Decision makers must have an experience base that allows them to recognize familiar aspects of a situation and what actions are likely to be effective. Similarly, they must be able to recognize that a specific situation is *not* familiar, that something is not quite right so they can investigate further before acting. Scenario-based training is one way to efficiently increase a learner's experience base; however, the learner must be actively engaged in the learning to receive the experiential benefits. The Scenario Immersion Principle increases the likelihood that learners will be cognitively and emotionally engaged in the learning experience.

The fact that augmented reality allows the learner to interact with the blended physical and virtual world in a realistic way, both increases the sense of immersion and also the learning value. Gibson (2000) emphasizes the importance of perception–action coupling in perceptual learning. In other words, if the learner receives feedback for actions in the training environment just as one would interacting in the real world, the links between specific perceptions and actions are strengthened. An immersive experience that includes realistic perception–action coupling is likely to readily generalize to real-world experiences.

3.1.5   Summary and Discussion

The Scenario Immersion Principle amplifies the value of scenario-based training for creating an immersive learning experience that leverages the sense of "being there" augmented reality fosters. Engagement and immersion are highly interrelated, so we draw from both literatures to explore strategies for increasing the learner's sense of presence in the learning experience. Both emotional and cognitive engagement are important components of immersion. Scenario-based training that incorporates augmented reality can evoke emotions one is likely to experience on the job, and also facilitate cognitive engagement in the form of active sensemaking and problem-solving. Factors that increase engagement and immersion include training that has personal relevance and meaning, links to prior knowledge and skills, an emphasis on learning-oriented goals (rather than focusing on performance goals exclusively), and a sense of mystery and surprise.

3.1.6   Implications for Training Design

The blended virtual–physical world created by augmented reality creates fertile ground for an immersive learning experience. Visual cues are the cornerstone of most augmented reality training applications. However, engaging more senses can increase the sense of immersion. There may be opportunities to incorporate audio, tactile, and olfactory cues. Realistic sounds such as sirens and radio communications; the smell of spent ammunition or blood; the feel of a patient's chest as it rises and falls (or doesn't) can all add to the sense of "being there." Deciding which sensory cues to include depends largely on the domain. Often background noises that are only tangentially relevant to the scenario such as the sound of a helicopter, people speaking, or the sounds of rain can increase immersion. For some learning objectives, it may be important to avoid breaking immersion. For example, if the goal is to provide learners practice at managing time stress and distractions. One way to incorporate training elements such as hints or probes without disrupting the sense of immersion is to use virtual team members to ask questions or provide direction.

✔ Consider incorporating sensory cues to enhance immersion (visual, auditory, tactile, and olfactory cues).
✔ In addition to cues that support learning objectives, consider sensory cues that increase cognitive and emotional engagement.
✔ Maintain a learner's immersion in the training by using virtual team members to insert learning probes or offer hints.

3.2   Hot Seat Principle

Hot Seat Principle. Creating a learning situation in which the learner feels responsible for managing the situation supports recognition skill development.

3.2.1   What Do We Mean by the Hot Seat?

We use the term "hot seat" to refer to the strategy of placing learners in challenging scenarios in which they must make sense of the situation and decide how to act to promote active engagement. Although immersion and active engagement may seem synonymous, it is possible for an experience to be immersive and for the learner to be passive. For example, a movie may be highly immersive. IMAX theaters and movies with 3D effects are designed to give the viewer that sense of "being there"; yet, the viewer is a passive recipient of the immersive media. The goal of the Hot Seat Principle is to increase engagement by creating an experience where learners believe they are responsible for making decisions. Being in the hot seat pushes the learner to actively participate in the scenario. Being in the hot seat makes it difficult to stay passive, absorbing information and waiting to see what happens next. Instead, learners know that they will be called on to commit to assessment and actions, raising their level of activation, engagement, and focus. For team training, being in the hot seat diminishes the sense of shared responsibility; when learners know the responsibility for resolving the situation lies with them, this changes the way they interact with the team. It reduces the likelihood that a learner will become detached from the training scenario or politely defer to other team members.

3.2.2 Why Is the Hot Seat Important?

Experienced instructors describe the importance of training strategies that keep the learner engaged in information gathering and problem-solving. These anecdotal reports are supported by research showing that training that keeps students mentally and physically active in the learning process – sometimes described as active learning – improves learning outcomes (Collins & O'Brien, 2003; Michael, 2006). Putting the learner in the hot seat is an effective strategy for promoting active learning; more so than training experiences in which learners observe others performing tasks. Being in the hot seat forces learners to construct their own meaning from the situation and take action. Scenario-based training in which the learner is responsible for decision-making provides an opportunity for learners to actively apply principles and concepts learned in the classroom, make mistakes, explore solutions, and receive feedback. Furthermore, being in the hot seat may evoke some of the same types of stress one would experience on the job. The sensation that others are relying on the learner to make decisions, time pressure, and uncertainty are examples of stressors that learners will have to manage in high-stakes environments. These stressors manifest in the real world in health care, military, firefighting, and many other domains with complex and dynamic conditions. Training that puts the learner in the hot seat provides an opportunity to practice recognizing these and other stressors, and develop strategies for working through them.

3.2.3 Examples and Empirical Support

Support for the Hot Seat Principle comes primarily from the experiences of skilled instructors. In some academic medical centers, this principle has been incorporated into resident physician training. Much of the practical hands-on training happens in small groups, where one learner is in the role of decision-maker and others observe. While much can be learned by observing others, it can be difficult to maintain attention. To aid with focus, some instructors use a rotating hot seat technique. Every learner knows that the hot seat could be handed to them at any point in the scenario when indicated by the instructor. This increases engagement by encouraging each resident to construct their own understanding of the situation and be prepared to act even when in observation mode.

Another strategy used in medical training that integrates the Hot Seat Principle is rapid cycle deliberate practice (Hunt et al., 2014). For this type of training, learners are asked to assess and treat a simulated patient. Learners are given direct feedback when an error occurs; at this point, the scenario rewinds and the learners have an opportunity to try again (and again!) until they master that particular skill component. The notion here is that the learner is in the hot seat until they master the skill. It is not enough to nod along in agreement when given feedback and imagine doing it better in the future; rather, the learner tries again until they get it right. An evaluation study of rapid cycle deliberate feedback with pediatric resident physicians learning resuscitation skills resulted in improvements in the quality of resuscitation efforts over residents who participated in traditional debrief sessions. Residents who participated in rapid cycle deliberate practice were more likely to initiate bag valve mask ventilation airway management, were faster to start chest compressions, and were more likely to start defibrillation within two minutes of a loss of pulse – all of which increase the likelihood of patient survival. The authors note that for this technique to be effective, learners must experience psychological safety. They describe how learners transitioned from "being nervous about making mistakes to being enthusiastic about the opportunity for dedicated coaching and practice time" (Hunt et al., 2014, p. 946). Psychological safety may be core to the effectiveness of the Hot Seat Principle. If learners are nervous or overwhelmed, they may have difficulty engaging with the training scenario.

A third example of the Hot Seat Principle was demonstrated in the context of sepsis recognition training for resident emergency department pediatricians (Geis et al., 2018). Researchers at Cincinnati Children's Hospital Medical Center conducted a cognitive task analysis to identify differences in resident (trainee) and experienced physician decision-making related to recognizing sepsis in children. They found that resident physicians were able to recount many of the same cues that experienced physicians did, but often deferred to more experienced team members to interpret the cues, anticipate how the situation would likely unfold, and determine appropriate actions. Upon reflection, faculty hypothesized that the on-the-job training in some ways cultivated this deference to more senior physicians; the resident is not generally the decision maker when it comes to patient care. In fact, relatively recent supervision rules were put in place to ensure that residents are not solely responsible for decisions about patient care. Supervision rules are designed to decrease the likelihood that patient care will be left in the hands of an inexperienced (and often exhausted) resident. However, this also means that resident physicians do not get an opportunity to practice being in the hot seat. To fill this gap, the faculty at Cincinnati Children's Hospital Medical Center developed simulation-based training that put resident physicians in the hot seat. In the safety of the simulation center, the residents were presented a patient and had no senior physicians available to consult with or defer to; rather, they were asked to assess the patient, determine which cues were relevant, interpret cues, and determine what actions to take.

A fourth example of the Hot Seat Principle was developed by Lia DiBello and her team at Applied Cognitive Sciences Lab Inc. (ACSI)(DiBello, 2018). ACSI develops virtual world exercises designed to help companies realign the skills of their senior teams to the evolving demands of the ever-changing business situations. In ACSI's Maxx virtual world, learners are dealing with changes in consumer markets. They are represented in the virtual world by an avatar. This serious game can be played as either an individual or a team. You (or your team) are senior leadership at Maxx, a company that is smaller than its competitors and losing its position in the marketplace. To win, you must develop a new product and launch it. Your product must be "game changing" and able to compete against numerous other consumer choices. The goal is to achieve a return on sales of 14 percent, while getting immediate "good-neutral-bad" feedback scores on every one of sixty decisions along the way, letting you (or your team) know how your thinking has affected sales. As expected, DiBello and her colleagues found that those who played as individuals found the experience more stressful than those who worked as part of a team. However, they were surprised to find that individuals performed significantly better than those who played as teams. All of the individual players met or exceeded the business goals for Maxx. Although they don't use the term "hot seat" in their interpretation of these findings, the explanation provided aligns with the Hot Seat Principle. They hypothe-size that individuals were more emotionally engaged than teams. One indicator is that DiBello and her team got phone calls from individual players, sometimes defending their actions when the game was giving them negative feedback on a specific decision. Individuals felt more account-able and were highly sensitive to feedback, all of which led to greater engagement and improved performance.

3.2.4 Links to Macrocognition

Being in the hot seat requires the learner to construct their own understanding of the situation and determine what actions to take. This type of meaning-making is one of the key components of recognition skills. The recognition-primed decision model (Klein et al., 1988) describes how experienced decision-makers are able to quickly size up a situation and know what to do. The Hot Seat Principle allows learners to practice these skills in a safe environment. Augmented reality training provides an opportunity to practice creating meaning and taking action in a range of situations even before one has the skill to effectively and safely manage these situations in the real world. These hot seat experiences add to the experience base needed for effective recognition-primed decisions.

The Hot Seat Principle is also compatible with the constructivist paradigm of education (Driver et al., 1994; Mayer, 2005; Michael, 2006). Constructivism emphasizes that knowledge cannot simply be transferred from one person to another; rather, the learner must construct meaning by leveraging information and models they already have and expanding them to include new information. Being in the hot seat forces learners out of a passive state. They must make meaning based on the information available and decide what to do. Feedback allows the learner to identify flaws in understanding and further improve on or elaborate mental models.

Augmented reality technology is well-suited to applying the Hot Seat Principle. It can be used to place the learner in a scenario where they must quickly assess the situation and decide how to act. Using either a head-worn or handheld device, the learner can explore the blended virtual–physical world from a first-person perspective that is difficult to achieve through a computer screen. Learners can move through the world to change their perspective, view virtual and physical objects from different positions, and manipulate physical objects as they would in the real world. The scenario can evolve, either in a predictable fashion or based on the learner's interventions. This realism, combined with the sense that others are relying on the learner to manage the challenges presented in the scenario to keep others safe, complete a mission, treat a patient, and so on, can create a powerful sense of engagement.

3.2.5 Summary and Discussion

The Hot Seat Principle refers to training that places the learner in the role of a decision-maker who must manage a challenging scenario. The goal of this principle is to promote active engagement. Both experienced instructors and researchers advocate for the value of keeping learners mentally and physically active in the learning process. The Hot Seat Principle makes it difficult for the learner to remain passive or defer to others. Being in the hot seat allows the learner to practice making decisions and experience the stress of time pressures, uncertainty, and responsibility in an immersive, but safe context. Applications of this principle can be found in the medical education training literature. We suspect that this principle is widely used in other domains where training is not as carefully documented. The Hot Seat Principle promotes meaning-making, one of the key components of recognition skills, and is also compatible with the constructivist paradigm of education. It creates a level of emotional and cognitive engagement that increases the likelihood of learning transfer to job performance.

Augmented reality technology allows training designers to put the learner in the hot seat in a highly realistic setting. Learners can explore the blended virtual–physical world to create their own understanding of the situation and determine how to act.

3.2.6   Implications for Training Design

The goal of the Hot Seat Principle is to create a situation in which the learner truly feels responsible for the scenario outcomes. It is especially useful for team-based learning experiences to prevent individuals from becoming disengaged due to a diffusion of responsibility among team members. For small group training, the notion that anyone can be called on to be in the "hot seat" at any time during the training scenario is one way to implement this principle. Regardless of whether training targets individuals, teams, or small groups, learners should feel that the training is preparing them to manage high-stakes situations in the real world. It should be clear that they are practicing not just to avoid pixels dying on the screen (for medical training), but to save lives when confronted with challenges on the job. Applying the Hot Seat Principle may include telling learners that they are the only ones available to respond to an incident. Even if in the real world there would typically be a more senior person in charge, the stage can be set so that the senior person is simply not available and therefore the team is depending on the learner to manage the situation. In medical simulations, learners are often told a senior clinician or a specialist is not immediately available or there are no operating rooms available when support is requested.

For the Hot Seat Principle to work well, the learner must feel a sense of psychological safety. To avoid learners becoming overwhelmed and paralyzed, it should be clear that they are participating in a learning experience, and that the intent is for them to practice, perhaps try new things, and receive constructive feedback within the safety of the simulation environment. There should be a clear signal when and if the situation switches to evaluation that may have implications for continuing in a training program, job promotion, and so on.

✔ Use deliberate strategies to create situations in which learners feel responsible for scenario outcomes. For example:
  ◦ For small group training, rotate who sits in the "hot seat" during training.
  ◦ When learners ask for additional resources and support, respond that other personnel are not available, resources are in use, and so on.
✔ Maintain psychological safety for learners so they understand they can make mistakes without negative repercussions for them.

CHAPTER 4

Scenario Building

The topic of scenario building could fill an entire handbook on its own. We do not attempt to be comprehensive; rather, we assume some knowledge and experience with scenario development and offer two principles particularly relevant for recognition skills training: the Periphery Principle and the Perturbation Principle. Both focus on moving beyond an idealized version of how a situation will present and unfold, and a rigid focus on standard operating procedures. These principles focus on creating training that will aid learners in developing the problem detection, attention management, and adaptation skills needed to operate effectively in dynamic and uncertain settings. Because scenario-building principles are difficult to consider in the abstract, we offer examples from our own work. We include examples of domain-specific critical cues and complexity factors that can be used to integrate peripheral cues and perturbations into training scenarios.

Cognitive task analysis is an important thread in this chapter. Identifying which cues to include in the blended virtual–physical world, and which complexities to include in training scenarios is not trivial. We find cognitive task analysis methods essential to eliciting challenging incidents from experienced practitioners to inform these aspects of training design.

We highlight how augmented reality technologies can present compelling training scenarios by:

- presenting critical cues that may be difficult to represent using other training technologies,
- using built-in gaze or eye tracking to monitor which cues the learner attends to,
- providing a rapid "reset" so that the learner can rework a scenario multiple times to explore how different adaptations may play out in a given scenario, and
- allowing for a range of hinting strategies to support learners in noticing critical cues and adapting to perturbations.

4.1 Periphery Principle

Periphery Principle. Effective scenarios should include critical cues that are not obvious; rather, the learner must know to look for them and correctly interpret them.

4.1.1 *What Do We Mean by Periphery?*

We use the term "periphery" to refer to the fact that in the real world, critical cues are not always in the center focus, obvious, or easily perceived. Training scenarios should provide practice in detecting and interpreting these peripheral, but important cues. In some cases, important cues may seem peripheral because there are more salient cues drawing your attention. For example, in combat medicine, critical cues may not always be the most attention-grabbing symptoms a patient presents. In fact, experienced personnel report that it is easy to get distracted by dramatic injuries to the face or head and fail to conduct a complete and timely assessment of other injuries. In other cases, cues may seem peripheral because they are easily overlooked. For example, in an interview with an experienced pararescue jumper, he recalled noticing that a road looked "too clean" just before an improvised explosive device went off. Of the many types of threats to watch for, a road that is too clean is easy to miss. In still other cases, critical cues may seem peripheral because they are subtle. Experienced medics may notice pallor and other changes in skin tone and affect that are difficult to detect if you do not have the experience base required to make these sometimes subtle perceptual discriminations.

Learning to look for and interpret seemingly peripheral cues is a necessary component of *problem detection*, the process by which people become aware that events may be taking an unexpected and undesirable direction (Klein et al., 2005). This can be particularly challenging to train because this type of skill is not generic; rather one must learn to notice cues and understand their significance in the context of a particular situation. Consider the following story from an interview with an experienced intensive care unit pediatrician:

> A two-year-old with a history of developmental delay was admitted to the pediatric intensive care unit with respiratory distress and pneumonia. The patient's respiratory symptoms continued to worsen. Overnight he developed wheezing and a fever and was soon intubated. When the pediatrician saw this patient the next morning after handoff from the night shift, he immediately noted that he was "not looking very well." During the handoff, the night shift team reported that they were very worried about his

respiratory symptoms and actively working on determining the cause of the symptoms to drive treatment. There was discussion of whether the symptoms were related to bronchospasm, and if they should administer albuterol, a quick relief medication used to treat wheezing and shortness of breath. The day shift pediatrician, however, noted that patient also had high fever and a high heart rate (tachycardia), important indicators of a life-threatening condition called sepsis. The night shift team was so focused on the respiratory symptoms that they did not recognize the larger problem that was developing. The day shift pediatrician ordered fluids and labs to test his suspicion that the patient had become septic, and to prevent decompensation. The patient responded to the fluids as expected, the labs further confirmed his suspicions, and the team shifted treatment focus to managing sepsis.

In this incident, the night shift team was so focused on the distressing (and distracting) respiratory symptoms that they failed to recognize the significance of the fever, rapid heart rate, and overall ill appearance, thereby delaying detection and treatment of sepsis. The Periphery Principle emphasizes creating scenarios that include distracting cues, easy-to-miss cues, and subtle cues to create scenarios that require the learner to notice and recognize seemingly peripheral cues.

4.1.2   Why Are Peripheral Cues an Important Component of Scenario Development?

For recognition skills acquired in training to transfer to job performance, learners must have an opportunity to practice them in contexts they are likely to face on the job. Including peripheral cues in training scenarios allows learners to practice attention management (Klein et al., 2003) as they learn to look beyond the most attention-grabbing cues, honing their problem-detection skills. Problem-detection skills are critical to recognizing errors and anticipating problems. The potential implications for performance are profound. Improved problem-detection skills lead to more timely and effective interventions and are critical to avoiding fixation. An interview with a helicopter pilot provides a vivid example:

> It was a night mission in Afghanistan in which they were doing a route scan of primary and auxiliary roads. The pilot was using night vision goggles to look for anything unusual. As he was flying along, he noticed a large blast crater from a previous explosion. There were three men working in the crater. It was not uncommon for people to do road work at night to avoid the heat of the sun. However, he knew from experience to

look around the crater to learn more about what was going on. He flew a big slow circle around them, turning gently to avoid slapping the air and creating a lot of noise with the rotor system. As he was circling, he scanned up and down the road, looking for sentries. He saw four people armed with machine guns he had not noticed initially. The men were positioned to the north, south, east, and west, each a couple of hundred meters away from the crater – clearly standing guard for the men working in the crater. As he examined the scene, he noticed a distinctive bag commonly used to hold the equipment needed to emplace an improvised explosive device. It became clear that these men were not doing road repairs; they were placing a bomb. He was able to alert ground forces to the bomb in the road and execute a hasty attack.

In this case, as the pilot examined the peripheral cues, the interpretation of the situation quickly changed from innocuous road work to a threat. Being able to distinguish friendly activities from enemy threats is critical for reconnaissance pilots. Peripheral cues often add some of the "messiness" of the real world; they may be easily missed or interpreted in a number of different ways. Training focuses on giving these pilots the experiences they need so that they can look beyond the obvious, to consider those peripheral cues that may mean the difference between a successful and an unsuccessful mission.

4.1.3 Examples and Empirical Support

To incorporate peripheral cues into training scenarios, training designers must consider the range of cues that may be relevant and their implications in a particular situation. One strategy for obtaining this information is to interview experienced practitioners using cognitive task analysis, a set of methods designed to elicit cognitive aspects of expertise in the context of challenging incidents (Crandall et al., 2006; Militello & Hoffman, 2008). This approach has been used to collect a case base of challenging incidents related to a particular disease or condition (Crandall & Getchell-Reiter, 1993; Militello & Lim, 1995; Patterson et al., 2016), or a specific type of military mission (Militello et al., 2019) to inform scenario development. Cognitive task analysis involves in-depth interviews that focus on unpacking each case to explore what the interviewee was paying attention to, what decisions they made, and how it could have occurred differently. After collecting a case base of challenging incidents, researchers can look across all cases to identify common themes, cues that are important, cues that are commonly missed, cues that are distracting, and subtle cues that may be difficult to discern. Incidents can also be analyzed to identify elements that increase complexity. Two important outputs from cognitive task analysis that can inform scenario design include an inventory of critical cues (Tables 4.1 and 4.2), and a complexities table (Table 4.3).

Table 4.1 *Necrotizing enterocolitis critical cue inventory*

Necrotizing Enterocolitis Indicators		
Early Gastrointestinal Cues	Infection Cues	Late Gastrointestinal Cues
Girth increase	Poor perfusion	Dramatic change in any of the early gastrointestinal cues
Aspirates	Color changes	
Guaiac positive stool	Change in activity level	Discolored abdomen
Loops	Increase in apneas/bradycardias	No bowel sounds
Emesis	Change in oxygen requirement	Abdomen is hard
	Temperature instability	Abdomen is tender
	Infant looks ill	Frank blood in stool

(adapted from Militello & Lim, 1995)

Table 4.2 *Distal perfusion critical cue inventory*

Poor Distal Perfusion Indicators			
Skin Color	Extremities	Temperature	Other
Pale	Mottled extremities	Cold	Delayed capillary refill
Paleish gray	Cold extremities	Sweating	Decreased peripheral perfusion
Pasty	Pale extremities	Perfusion is warm	
Pallor	Yellowish nose		Poor peripheral pulses
Yellowish			Vasoconstriction
No nice flush on cheeks			Thready pulses
Mottled			
Flushed			
Purple			
Reticulated pattern			

(adapted from Patterson et al., 2016)

Table 4.3 *Excerpt from complexities table for Army Aviation reconnaissance missions illustrating opportunities to introduce peripheral cues*

Complexity	Description/Elaboration
1. Multiple sources of data coming into the cockpit	Increasingly sophisticated sensors and automation lead to more information sources, creating challenges for attention management, integration, and analysis. This includes networked systems from multiple domains including air, land, maritime, space, and cyberspace.
2. "Soda straw" effect	Looking through sensors may be "like looking through a soda straw" (keyhole effect).
3. Multiple entities may need to be located and tracked simultaneously	Sometimes reconnaissance may identify multiple subjects of interest that may be moving in different directions. This may require tracking multiple entities simultaneously.
4. Enemy uses decoys	Enemy uses decoys to misdirect. This creates a need to expend attentional and physical resources to distinguish decoys from actual targets. Distinguishing decoys from actual targets requires use of multiple sensors providing views from multiple angles. This can include integrating views from an unmanned aerial system (UAS) above with views from own sensors.
5. Enemy employs camouflage and deception	In one case, the enemy combatants wore uniforms that from a distance appeared to be host country police.
6. Enemy vs. non-enemy entities may have similar sensor signatures	In some cases, it will be difficult to distinguish the sensory system indicators of enemy entities (vehicles, aircraft, soldiers) from non-enemy entities (civilian, own forces, friendly forces). "For the guys in Germany and Poland, our allies there use Russian equipment, painted a different color and pointed in a different direction. Good guy T-72 versus Bad guy T-72." (Interviewee)
7. Enemy and non-enemy may be difficult to discriminate	It can be a challenge to discriminate "threat" from "non-threat" behavior. For example, distinguishing individuals laying an improvised explosive device from individuals working to fix the road can sometimes be a challenge requiring more context and knowledge of normal life behavior.

(adapted from Militello et al., 2019)

A critical cue inventory details the cues described across cases. For example, in a study of recognition skills for necrotizing enterocolitis in premature infants, researchers created the critical cue inventory depicted in Table 4.1. Because necrotizing enterocolitis is an infection of the bowel, cues include both indicators of gastrointestinal distress and infection. Some are obvious and routinely measured such as an increase in abdominal girth and emesis (vomiting); others are easier to overlook such as poor distal perfusion (blood flow to extremities) and changes in activity level. Elements in this critical cue inventory can be used in different combinations to create training scenarios that leverage the Periphery Principle.

Table 4.2 depicts a more granular critical cue inventory. In a study of sepsis recognition in children, researchers identified twenty-four cues that were mentioned in descriptions of poor distal perfusion across twenty-three incidents, some more obvious than others. Because poor distal perfusion is an important indicator of sepsis in children, it is important that trainees learn to recognize it even when cues are subtle in comparison to other aspects of the patient's condition. Checking for delayed capillary refill by pressing the nail bed and monitoring how quickly the skin color returns is a standard strategy for assessing distal perfusion, but this is not always easily interpreted. Interviewees described many other cues they noticed as they described children they had treated. Incorporating these peripheral cues became a focus of a successful series of training scenarios for residents at Cincinnati Children's Hospital Medical Center (Geis et al., 2018). While many of these cues are difficult to represent on a manikin, simulation-center faculty introduced creative strategies such as putting the manikin's feet on ice prior to the simulation session so they would feel cold to the touch and showing videos of capillary refill so learners could practice distinguishing healthy from delayed refill.

A second output from cognitive task analysis is a complexities table, used to document contextual factors that increase complexity, including factors that make cue recognition difficult. Table 4.3 depicts a portion of a complexities table abstracted from an analysis of a case base of reconnaissance incidents as recalled by US Army helicopter pilots. The complexities in the left column represent factors that created challenges for pilots in accurately assessing the situation and taking appropriate action. The column on the right includes more detail, including why the complexity factor makes it difficult to recognize and interpret critical cues. This table was developed to inform a number of activities including making determinations about crewing, informing the design of human-machine teaming, and guiding the design of training scenarios (Militello et al., 2019). Scenario designers can refer to this table to incorporate contextual elements that will introduce complexities relevant to specific learning objectives. For example, Row 2 of

Table 4.3 refers to the fact that reconnaissance pilots looking at a sensor view literally have no peripheral view; it is as if one were looking through a soda straw. It is critical that training scenarios include important cues that extend beyond a single focus so that pilots learn to scan for relevant information in the area outside the initial focus. Learning to scan using a sensor view requires a specialized skill set that includes recognizing an anomaly and knowing where to look and what to look for in the surrounding area to accurately interpret the situation.

Tables 4.1, 4.2, and 4.3 provide examples of artifacts from projects that began by first understanding a range of cues and complexities that could then be combined in different ways to create scenarios that emphasize the inclusion of both central and peripheral cues. Another more streamlined approach is to work with a skilled practitioner(s) to develop a training scenario based on a critical event. This approach is often used in hospital systems after an adverse event (or near miss). Similarly, in many settings "war stories" provide the basis of training scenarios (Hu et al., 2012; Newsome et al., 2020). Training designers often work with skilled practitioners to adapt these real-life incidents into training scenarios, making judgments about which central, obvious cues and which more subtle, peripheral cues to include. The applied cognitive task analysis suite of methods (Militello & Hutton, 1998) was designed to aid Navy Instructional Systems Designers as they work with experienced Navy personnel to translate sea stories into powerful training scenarios that present realistic challenges and support critical cue recognition and interpretation (Militello et al., 1997). Eliciting and unpacking these peripheral cues and incorporating them into training can make the difference between a superficial training scenario and one that will prepare learners for the real world.

Because augmented reality makes it possible to display life-sized virtual people, equipment, and contextual elements, it is well-suited to supporting the Periphery Principle. The simulation can present a broad range of both central and peripheral cues, tailored to the training scenario. To increase difficulty, an instructor can use augmented reality to make the peripheral cues subtle or combine them with irrelevant or distracting cues. Conversely, an instructor can make peripheral cues more noticeable over time if the learner misses them initially. In medical simulation, some instructors report that they will increase the salience of specific cues until the learner notices, and then use the delayed recognition as a teaching point during the debrief. During a scenario, the instructor may increase the patient's blood pressure until the learner notices the problem, and then in the debrief highlight when the blood pressure first became a concern in relation to when the learner first noticed it. Augmented reality supports this technique for a range of cues that may be difficult to simulate over time with a physical manikin. For example, a virtual patient can become increasingly pale or flushed over time; the patient's expression can be relatively calm and then become panicked as breathing becomes difficult; eyes may be initially alert, but begin to look unfocused, or close altogether as the patient's mental status deteriorates over time.

4.1.4   *Links to Macrocognition*

One of the key components of recognition skills is knowing what to attend to, and determining which cues are relevant. This is challenging because which cues are relevant varies based on the situation. Furthermore, some critical cues may be attention grabbing, while others are less obvious and peripheral. The data-frame model of sensemaking describes how skilled practitioners sometimes notice peripheral cues that inexperienced people do not. In other situations, inexperienced people may notice important peripheral cues, but fail to understand their implications. Creating training scenarios that provide practice at identifying and interpreting peripheral cues critical to accurate assessment and appropriate intervention is a necessary component of recognition skills training.

4.1.5   *Summary and Discussion*

The Periphery Principle supports the first component of recognition skill, knowing what to attend to. This principle highlights the importance of incorporating peripheral cues into training scenarios so that learners can practice attention management skills as they learn to look beyond the most obvious, attention-grabbing cues to conduct a thorough and timely assessment. This practice can lead to improved problem detection and reduced fixation.

Developing training scenarios that incorporate peripheral cues is not always straightforward. This generally requires working with skilled practitioners. Sometimes this takes the form of a systematic cognitive task analysis to create a critical cue inventory and complexities table that can be used to inform a range of scenarios. In other cases, training designers work with skilled practitioners to turn a specific incident into a training scenario. In the latter case, cognitive task analysis techniques may be streamlined and used to help the skilled practitioner(s) unpack subtle, peripheral cues and their implications so they can be effectively incorporated into the training scenario.

The Periphery Principle is relevant for scenario-based training, regardless of the training platform. However, augmented reality may provide an advantage in some domains as some subtle peripheral cues may be difficult to represent using other training technologies. Augmented reality also makes it possible to display dynamic cues such as changes in skin tone and facial expression over time, changes in the sound of an approaching helicopter, and changes in the look of a piece of equipment as it malfunctions or degrades. Some augmented reality hardware can track learners' gaze patterns. This can help instructors evaluate whether learners looked at a visual cue to support real-time coaching and debrief discussions about critical cues.

4.1.6 Implications for Training Design

Incorporating peripheral cues into training requires designers to think beyond training the most salient set of cues. Designers should think about factors that will make it hard for learners to recognize and interpret cues in real-world contexts. Recreating the conditions that make it difficult to accurately assess a situation in the real world will help learners adapt as needed when confronted with challenging situations.

Determining which and how many peripheral cues to include can be difficult. Cognitive task analysis can help training designers determine which cues are relevant, which ones are important distractors, and which are confusing or easy to miss. Critical cue inventories and tables of complexity factors can be useful tools.

When working with skilled practitioners to create a critical cue inventory, we often ask questions such as: *Where do new people go wrong? Can you remember a time early in your career when you missed something important?* Sometimes these questions reveal cues that are not usually explicitly trained, but that skilled practitioners have learned to recognize. Often, they are an afterthought, the skilled practitioner may not have consciously considered these peripheral cues or talked about them frequently. Other times, they are "tricks of the trade" that experienced people share. Either way, eliciting these from the skilled practitioners can make the difference between superficial and compelling training scenarios.

> ✔ Incorporate cues that are sometimes difficult to detect, easily confused, or commonly overlooked into training scenarios.
> ✔ Incorporate complexity factors that make it harder to identify cues into training scenarios.
> ✔ Use cognitive task analysis to collect real-world incidents to identify relevant and compelling peripheral cues and complexities.

4.2   Perturbation Principle

Perturbation principle. Training scenarios should expose trainees to novel conditions requiring adaptation and performance under non-routine conditions.

4.2.1   *What Do We Mean by Perturbations?*

A perturbation is a deviation from the standard, a disruption of some kind. Some have described perturbations as curve balls, surprises, or roadblocks. Incorporating perturbations into training means the training designer purposely adds novel or unexpected events into training scenarios to provide practice at adaptation, and to support mental model development. For example, in medical training, a perturbation could involve a patient that has atypical anatomy or has a rare, adverse reaction to a treatment regimen. An environmental perturbation in health care might be caring for patients on respirators during a natural disaster that has affected the infrastructure causing equipment malfunction and/or scarcity of resources. Other examples include equipment malfunctions that require a pilot to troubleshoot while maintaining safe flight and managing a mission; or combat rescue crews receiving a call that there are three injured people only to find that there are five injured people when they arrive. Perturbations are the norm in many high-stakes environments. For training designers, often the challenge is less about identifying potential perturbations with training value and more about choosing which to include in limited training time.

4.2.2   *Why Are Perturbations Important in Training Scenarios?*

Trainees will get a real and productive workout if they must face scenarios with non-routine conditions, forcing them to adapt and move out of their comfort zone. Military trainers talk about learning to "adapt and overcome." As learners become more proficient in how a process normally unfolds or a system normally operates, it is important to start introducing perturbations to help stretch their abilities and provide opportunities to apply concepts in different ways. This is particularly important for domains characterized by uncertainty and rapidly changing conditions. It is not enough to know how to assess and treat a patient in a clean, controlled environment. A combat medic must be prepared to do this when equipment malfunctions or supplies are unavailable, when injuries appear in unusual combinations and when team members and a higher level of care are out of reach. Training scenarios must represent situations in which the standard operating procedures will not be sufficient; rather, the practitioner must adapt and improvise.

4.2.3 Examples and Empirical Support

Gorman and colleagues (2010) describe a perturbation training program aimed at training adaptive teams. They designed a perturbation training program and recruited university students to serve on three-person teams, learning to control simulated unmanned aerial systems to test the training program. The perturbation training consisted of a PowerPoint training on the history and current use of unmanned aerial vehicles (UAVs), followed by a brief training mission and training on the communications system in which participants learned to identify the source of static in the communication system and use multiple communication paths. Trainees then completed four training missions, three of which introduced different types of perturbations such as new target restrictions, new airspeed/altitude of target, and communication malfunctions. The fifth mission was an evaluation, designed to test the team's ability to perform under novel conditions by introducing a roadblock. Completing Mission 5 concluded the first session. Teams then returned after eight to ten weeks to complete three additional test missions that included a range of perturbations. Teams that received the perturbation training were compared to teams who received training that focused on cross-training or procedures. The cross-training and procedural training included similar training including the PowerPoint materials and four training missions but without exposure to training on troubleshooting static in the communication system or the perturbations in the training missions. They found that teams that received perturbation training performed better on the test mission at the end of session 1 (Mission 5) and also on two of the three test

Table 4.4 *Excerpt from complexities table for Army Aviation reconnaissance missions illustrating potential perturbations*

Complexity	Description/Elaboration
Degraded visual environment	Aircraft will operate under degraded visual conditions (e.g., clouds, fog, snow, dust) both at altitude and on takeoff/landing.
Degraded communications	This can be deliberate by enemy forces or a latent effect of a congested spectrum. Degradation may result in intermittent or sustained duration loss of communication.
GPS jamming by enemy forces	Jamming of GPS signal by enemy forces thereby degrading the quality of position, navigation, and timing. This may impact inputs to systems reliant on GPS.
Degraded sensors	The effectiveness of some sensors may degrade under certain conditions and may create challenges for automated systems such as autopilot functions.
Crew member becomes incapacitated	This will require someone else to take over the tasks. Furthermore, may need to deal with the loss of the aircraft if that aircraft needs to return to base to save the life of the incapacitated crew member, or because some weapons systems can only be operated from the seat of the incapacitated crew member.
Need for an unexpected landing	Completing an unplanned landing to conserve fuel while in a hostile environment introduces the need to balance accident risk (crashing while landing, unable to take back off) with mission risk (not having enough fuel to remain in the engagement zone to support the troops on the ground when it is needed, or the landed aircraft may get targeted by enemy forces further complicating the mission).
Aircraft malfunction	An aircraft malfunction arises during a mission that requires detection, diagnosis, and determining actions to be taken (e.g., abort, continue . . .).
Someone is injured and needs to be evacuated	Injured personnel requiring immediate medical attention introduces competing goals – saving the wounded individual versus accomplishing the mission.
One aircraft becomes incapacitated	If one aircraft becomes incapacitated (e.g., crashes) then another aircraft in that group needs to take over the tasks/functions of the incapacitated aircraft.

(adapted from Militello et al., 2019)

missions in the second session. The authors concluded that perturbation training allowed teams to develop the skills needed to adapt to novel conditions because they were forced to improvise during the training missions.

The notion of including perturbations in training is intuitively appealing. However, determining what perturbations to include can be challenging. Scenario designers can work with skilled practitioners using cognitive task analysis methods to identify perturbations that occur in the real world (Crandall et al., 2006; Militello & Hoffman, 2008). Table 4.4 depicts another portion of the complexities table abstracted from the analysis of reconnaissance incidents presented in Table 4.3 (see Section 4.1). Note that the complexities described in this table were described by US Army helicopter pilots as they recounted challenging incidents they had experienced over the course of their careers (Militello et al., 2019). These types of perturbations can be introduced into training scenarios to aid learners in practicing adaptation skills in a safe training environment.

Augmented reality training can facilitate the efficient introduction of perturbations. A small set of core scenarios can be edited to introduce different perturbations. This may allow for rapid generation of new scenarios based on world events such as an emerging enemy threat, or recent insights into technology limitations. As new challenges emerge, scenarios representing specific perturbations can be implemented throughout an organization to quickly disseminate lessons learned. Rather than relying on word-of-mouth and message boards, highly relevant perturbations and strategies for managing them can be disseminated in a standardized way. With other training media, hypothetical questions are often used to encourage the learner to mentally simulate perturbations. With augmented reality, the learner can actually replay a scenario with different perturbations, increasing realism and supporting practice at adapting to the demands of each perturbation. With regard to the instructional approach, an augmented reality platform can incorporate hints in the form of a visual pointer or a virtual colleague to support learners in managing perturbations. (See Section 7.1 for more discussion of the use of hints and prompts in training.)

4.2.4   *Links to Macrocognition*

The recognition-primed decision model suggests that skilled practitioners notice aspects of a novel situation that match previous experience. If the match is a close-enough approximation, the decision maker can implement actions and maintain expectations about how the new situation should unfold, based on what has happened in the past. Sometimes, however, a new situation may appear to be unprecedented, and the expert has no prior experience that matches it exactly. In that case, it is important to have *adaptive expertise*, in which the expert is able to apply knowledge and skills in novel ways (Ward et al., 2018). By inserting perturbations into training scenarios, learners become familiar with the skills associated with applying learned concepts in novel ways. This might involve understanding the concepts enough to recognize when they might or might not apply, developing expectations to support evaluating whether the standard procedure is an effective approach to dealing with the situation, and combining disparate methods to piece together an effective solution. This ability to *adapt* knowledge and skills to novel situations is a hallmark of skilled performance.

4.2.5   *Summary and Discussion*

Including perturbations is an important component of scenario-based training. The Perturbation Principle is focused on training learners to adapt. The principle supports two underlying components of recognition skills: knowing what to attend to and evaluating. Introducing unexpected deviations in training scenarios can make learners more nimble by teaching them to recognize which elements of the situation might be affected by a perturbation (knowing what to attend to), and to anticipate how the perturbation might affect the evolving situation (evaluating). Perturbation training has been shown to be effective in helping people better perform when unexpected events occur during a situation, likely because it teaches learners how to apply their knowledge in novel ways. Training designers can work with skilled practitioners to create a compilation of incidents in which disturbances affected situations to inform the design of training scenarios that include realistic perturbations.

Incorporating perturbations into training has several potential benefits. Perturbations are likely to introduce risk and degrade performance, particularly for less-skilled personnel. Simulation training provides a safe environment in which to fail without danger to patients, injury to oneself, or damage to expensive equipment. With augmented reality training, perturbations can be added by changing the virtual assets (e.g., presenting a patient with atypical anatomy), or by changing environmental elements (e.g., restricting the resources available). Augmented reality makes it relatively easy to "reset" the scene so the learner can go back and rework the scenario, exploring different adaptations to determine which are effective and which are not in the face of specific perturbations.

Determining which perturbations to include in training scenarios and at what stage of skill development requires both identifying realistic perturbations and understanding what types of complexity they introduce. It is important to include realistic perturbations so that learners understand that the training is intended to prepare them for challenges they will likely face and not an artificial exercise in which they are unfairly tricked. In some contexts, it may make sense to provide hints or other types of coaching to aid learners in adapting to specific types of perturbations. Using an augmented reality platform, it is possible to develop scenarios with a range of perturbations for rapid dissemination of standardized lessons learned across an organization, replay scenarios with different perturbations, and incorporate hints to help learners manage the perturbations.

4.2.6   *Implications for Training Design*

When working with skilled practitioners to identify important perturbations, they may be resistant. Often these details are linked with tacit knowledge and are difficult to recall. Furthermore, traditional training approaches focus on training standard procedures so skilled practitioners may have difficulty understanding the value of discussing perturbations in a training context.

Cognitive task analysis interviews often include probes such as: "Tell me about a time when your skills were challenged," or "Tell me about a time when someone with less experience may not have handled the situation as well as you did." If common perturbations are known, the interviewer might ask directly: "*Tell me about a time when communications equipment failed.*"

The goal is to elicit real-world examples that can be adapted and combined to create compelling training scenarios. However, it is not enough to elicit perturbations, it is also important to understand how skilled practitioners interpret and act in the face of perturbations. This may involve creating a scenario and asking several skilled practitioners to review and respond with their interpretation and recommended actions to create an expert model.

✔ Perturbations are unexpected roadblocks that force learners to adapt (e.g., equipment failures).
✔ Cognitive task analysis methods can help elicit potential perturbations from domain experts.
✔ Real-world examples of perturbations can be adapted and combined to create training scenarios.
✔ To provide useful feedback to learners, understand how domain experts would deal with the perturbations used in training scenarios.

CHAPTER 5

Fidelity and Realism

When designing training, focus on representing the most important cues accurately. The challenge is often in determining which are the most important cues and finding creative, practical ways to represent them accurately. Fidelity and realism are important considerations in training design and have been written about and researched extensively (Hays & Singer, 2012; Roza, 2004). Simulators, live actors, moulage (the use of makeup and other props to create realistic-looking injuries on live actors and manikins), and other ingenious techniques have been used to increase realism in training. In early simulation-based training efforts, there was a strong focus on "high fidelity," or efforts to make the simulated experience map as closely onto the real world as possible. In recent years, however, we have seen a shift in the conversation to a more nuanced consideration of what types of fidelity are important for specific training objectives. As Lintern and Boot (2021) posit: "It is not the degree to which the training and transfer tasks share features . . . , but the degree to which they share *critical* features . . . " (italics added, p. 543). In calling out *critical* features, Lintern and Boot identify the importance of certain features of a domain that will yield better transfer from training to on-the-job performance. For example, if the objective of a training program is to teach strategizing for military personnel, a tabletop exercise with realistic scenarios can be an effective training environment without the need to simulate an operations center completely. Creating a simulation environment that closely mimics the work environment is an added expense that is not critical to training key skills in some types of military strategizing. For training recognition skills, the concept of critical features builds on the work of E. J. Gibson (1969) who proposed that training that focuses on key cues and patterns (referred to as *invariants*) will support the learner in making important perceptual discriminations. Furthermore, training that conceals or distorts key cues and patterns can actually impede learning. For domains in which recognition skills are important to learn, training should prioritize the important cues and represent them as realistically as possible to improve transfer from training to on-the-job performance. For example, when learning how to recognize subtle signs of infection, training that allows learners to practice seeing the subtle signs of infection is more effective than training in which learners see a manikin without any indication of change in condition.

Because no simulated training experience can replicate everything about the real-world experience, training developers must determine what types of fidelity will most benefit the learner. Does the training need to be visually realistic? Will it help to incorporate high-fidelity auditory cues or even certain odors? Are there cognitive activities that must be incorporated, such as problem-solving and strategizing? Identifying the critical features to include in training requires careful analysis of the task to understand the key cues and patterns to be trained. Armed with this knowledge, training developers often find themselves exploring trade-offs in terms of cost, computational power, and other pragmatic concerns as they seek to maximize aspects of fidelity that align with training objectives.

In the context of augmented reality, we consider three design principles relevant to fidelity and realism in recognition skills training. The Sensory Fidelity Principle supports the development of perceptual skills critical to rapid and accurate assessments and actions. The Scaling Fidelity Principle provides practice at body positioning and managing spatial relationships. The Assessment–Action Pairing Principle allows learners to practice attention management and coordination skills that will be needed in the real world where assessing and acting are inextricably linked. Modern augmented reality technologies provide an opportunity to instantiate these three principles with more flexibility than ever before.

5.1   Sensory Fidelity Principle

Sensory Fidelity Principle. Realistic cue presentation is needed to support perceptual skill development.

5.1.1   *What Do We Mean by Sensory Fidelity?*

In a general sense, fidelity refers to how accurately specific aspects of the training experience represent their real-world counterparts. There are many kinds of fidelity to be considered in training development. For example, task fidelity, psychological fidelity, and cognitive fidelity refer to how well the training represents the task, psychological stressors, and cognitive challenges as they occur in the real world. (See Hays & Singer [2012] for an in-depth treatment of simulation fidelity.) In this discussion of recognition skills training, our interest is in sensory fidelity, or how realistically specific perceptual cues are represented in a training environment. When incorporating sensory fidelity into training, one goal is to create a learning situation in which learners use their own senses to gather information from the environment as they would on the job. For example, in a medical simulation, a scenario in which the patient's appearance is verbally described to learners as "pallor with eyes closed" has lower sensory fidelity than one in which learners view a virtual or real patient and make their own assessments about skin tone and mental status. Sensory fidelity could include visual, auditory, olfactory, and tactile elements.

It is important to note that discussion of fidelity is often complicated by conflating *high fidelity* with *high-tech*. Fidelity can be achieved in many ways, such as by using highly realistic virtual environments, simulators, actors, moulage, or realistic tabletop exercises. It is possible to have high-fidelity cues in low-tech environments and vice versa. In medical training, a cadaver has very high fidelity with respect to anatomy, and is also very low-tech. Low-tech, text-based simulations can feel more realistic and even induce stress for first responders if high-fidelity sounds such as recordings of sirens or helicopters are present. Conversely, high-tech manikins that do not accurately represent human anatomy should be considered low fidelity and actually have negative training outcomes for some learning objectives.

Determining the type and level of fidelity to be used in training nearly always requires trade-offs. For example, it may be hard to achieve both functional fidelity (realistic interactions and functions) and sensory fidelity. Using live actors with moulage allows for realistic interactions with the patient, but lower fidelity with regard to injury states, illnesses, and vital signs. With live actors, it is difficult to create high-fidelity representations of many conditions such as changes in skin tone, fever, or elevated blood pressure. Using videos of actual patients may provide more sensory fidelity so the learner can see realistic wounds, blood flow, flushed skin, and agitation or altered mental status. One trade-off with videos, however, is that videos provide very low interaction fidelity – learners cannot examine the patient or ask the patient questions. Another trade-off to consider when making fidelity decisions is about development versus implementation costs. For example, using human actors (called standardized patients in health-care simulations) with moulage incurs relatively low development costs but may be more expensive to implement in terms of coordination and labor costs. Similarly, for military aviators, flying training missions in helicopters has low development costs, but is expensive in terms of fuel, aircraft maintenance, and coordination. Augmented reality training may require a larger investment up front during development, but after it has been developed, it can be implemented widely. These are just a few examples of the types of trade-offs training developers weigh; there are many others that will arise depending on training domains and goals. To many trade-offs, there are many examples of creative hybrid approaches in which training developers integrate multiple training approaches into a single training experience. For example, medical students may be asked to assess a live actor to determine the need for intubation and then perform the intubation on a manikin.

For a focus on recognition skills training, augmented reality allows for high sensory fidelity in terms of photorealistic visual cues, realistic audio cues, and appropriate scaling. For example, augmented reality developers working with skilled medical illustrators, are able to create virtual patients that allow learners to visually inspect wounds that appear as they would on actual patients. Augmented reality software allows for the presentation of photorealistic 3D views of wounds, facial expressions, skin conditions (e.g., flushing, rashes), equipment (e.g., monitoring devices), and nearly anything else – limited primarily by bandwidth and processing power. If a virtual patient is life-sized, learners can walk around the virtual patient to conduct an examination; they can look more closely at a specific part of the anatomy, listen to breath sounds, and observe the rise and fall of the chest. This ability to move in the environment allows learners to practice assessing the whole patient in a manner similar to the way they would on the job, changing what they perceive by moving their bodies in relation to virtual assets. The combination of highly realistic perceptual cues and appropriate scaling increases sensory fidelity in a manner that is difficult to replicate with other training media. (See Section 5.2 for additional discussion of this component.)

However, if relying on a virtual patient exclusively, the training would be low in tactile fidelity. The addition of a physical manikin to the training environment can be used to increase tactile and functional fidelity. Similarly, it is possible to increase olfactory fidelity by adding scents. The ability to query the patient can be simulated using natural language processing algorithms to cue recorded or computer-generated patient responses, further increasing functional fidelity with more realistic interactions, but also adding expense and development complexity. Training designers must determine which types of cues are critical to the learning objectives and make trade-offs based on training priorities and resources available. (See Chapter 4 on Scenario Development for discussion of cognitive task analysis for determining which cues to include.) For example, training communication skills in health-care workers will require higher realism in terms of patient interactions, whereas when making accurate assessments and diagnosis of patient condition is the main focus of a training exercise, sensory and tactile realism should be prioritized. Notably, the cost to create augmented reality training may be greater initially than recruiting, training, and applying moulage to live actors, but the resulting augmented reality training can be used repeatedly across different settings.

5.1.2   Why Does Sensory Fidelity Matter?

There is a well-documented phenomenon in which students emerge from training with their heads full of declarative and procedural knowledge but are still faced with the task of learning how to apply such knowledge in real-world tasks (Benner, 1984; Dreyfus & Dreyfus, 1980). A critical component of becoming a proficient practitioner in any domain is learning to recognize patterns and anomalies. In complex environments such as health care, clinicians are bombarded with information and interruptions that compete for their attention. They must learn what to attend to, the implications of specific patterns, how to recognize weak signals (i.e., often subtle indicators of potential problems), and how to make sense of seemingly conflicting information. Kellman and Krasne (2018) describe this challenge as it relates to the transition from medical school to in-hospital learning:

> Students who have been carefully taught and who have diligently absorbed declarative and procedural inputs fail to recognize key structures and patterns in real-world tasks, such as interpreting radiographs, ECGs, cytology, and other clinical images and tests. Trainees may know procedures but fail to understand their conditions of application or which ones apply to new problems or situations. And learners may understand but process slowly, with high cognitive load, causing them to be impaired in demanding, complex, or time-limited tasks. In the realm of medicine, there is clearly a gap between the foundational knowledge gained in medical school and the ability to recognize relevant, clinical patterns during residency and beyond. (Kellman & Krasne, 2018, p. 2)

This effect, known as the "July effect," has been studied in the context of resident physicians in the United States where residencies begin in July (Young et al., 2011). As a result, hospitals get an influx of resident physicians freshly launched from medical school and ready to apply what they have learned each July. Studies show that in the weeks following the introduction of new resident physicians, hospital systems experience increased mortality rates and decreased efficiency of care. To explore the magnitude of the problem Young and colleagues (2011) conducted a careful meta-analysis of published studies on this topic. They found that studies on this topic varied considerably in their methodological rigor, so they focused on studies that had adequate sample sizes and adequate controls for comparison. Of these higher-quality studies, 45 percent reported statistically significant high mortality during July with effect sizes ranging from a relative risk increase of 4.3–12 percent. Thirty-seven percent of the high-quality studies reported a decrease in efficiency (e.g., length of stay, hospital charges, etc.) with effect sizes ranging from 0.3–7.2 percent compared to other months or nonteaching hospitals, or both. In response, many academic medical centers have created sophisticated simulation facilities that provide resident physicians an opportunity to practice on realistic manikins in a simulated clinical setting with the same monitors and medical equipment they use on the job. The intent is to provide a learning experience that includes sensory fidelity so that resident physicians can practice recognizing relevant clinical patterns for critical conditions in a safe environment where they receive real-time feedback from experienced physicians.

5.1.3 Examples and Empirical Support

Without first-hand experience observing and interpreting sensory cues, it is very difficult to obtain the perceptual skills needed to recognize patterns. Flashcard-type training interventions can support pattern recognition skill development when they (1) depict critical cues with high sensory fidelity, (2) ask the learner to form an assessment, and (3) provide feedback. Scenario-based training that embeds high sensory fidelity critical cues in realistic scenarios goes a step further, promoting development of sense-making skills by providing practice at distinguishing relevant cues from distractors, recognizing weak but important signals and peripheral cues, and considering the implications of specific patterns in a larger context.

In the context of aviation decision-making, Wiggins and O'Hare (2003) created Weatherwise, a cue-based trainer that exemplifies both the flashcard-type training and scenario-based training. The goal of the trainer was to aid pilots in recognizing deteriorating weather conditions that warrant a diversion from planned flights. Working with subject-matter experts, the designers of the training program identified nine visual cues that are critical indicators of deterioration of weather to the point of rendering further visual flight dangerous. The designers further identified that the presence of three or more of these cues indicates the point at which further visual flight should be discontinued. The training program focuses on teaching learners to recognize these nine cues.

The Weatherwise training proceeds in four stages. During the first stage, trainees are presented with visual in-flight images (out-of-the-window view from the pilot's perspective) and are required to assess if the conditions are above or below the minimum requirements for visual flight. The next stage focuses specifically on the nine cues. Trainees are presented with in-flight images of weather conditions that vary the nine cues: cloudbase, visibility, cloud coloring, terrain clearance, rain, horizon, cloud type, wind direction, and wind speed. The images include annotations about particular visual weather cues that trainees can access by placing the cursor over various parts of the image. During the third stage of training, learners are presented with in-flight images of deteriorating weather conditions and asked to state the extent to which they perceive each cue to be significant. In the final stage of training, learners are presented with in-flight video recordings and asked to identify the point in the video when weather conditions deteriorated below the requirements for visual flight rules. Learners receive feedback on their decisions. An evaluation study using sixty-six licensed private pilots showed promising results for this training approach. Control group pilots who did not receive Weatherwise training were significantly more likely to continue a simulated flight in deteriorating weather conditions than those who received Weatherwise training (Wiggins & O'Hare, 2003).

Weatherwise illustrates the Sensory Fidelity Principle by using high-fidelity in-flight images, which allow trainees to practice using the same sense that they would use in the real world (their vision) to notice the relevant cues. One strength of Weatherwise is that it proactively prepares the learner by providing an overview of the nine cues, and then prompts the learner to identify them in context of images of in-flight conditions and provides feedback. By exposing learners to high-fidelity patterns and images, they can begin to form an accurate mental model of important cues and how their meaning changes based on the context in which they appear (Salas et al., 2001) *before* they begin applying them in a scenario. Thus, mental model preparation may enhance the power of the Sensory Fidelity Principle. (See Section 6.1.)

Kellman and Krasne (2018) combined perceptual learning (e.g., Gibson, 1969) with adaptive learning to create an online tool to train complex pattern recognition skills in certain medical interpretation tasks (e.g., radiology, pathology, ultrasound, etc.). Using learners' speed and accuracy in responding to realistic images, the Perceptual and Adaptive Learning Modules (PALMs) adapted to learners' performance in real time. The PALMs could show more images that learners interpreted incorrectly (or slowly) until learners responded to them appropriately. Kellman and Krasne present findings on one type of PALM (interpreting electrocardiogram morphology), showing that novices experienced significant improvements in both accuracy and fluency of identifying target images. Third-year medical students improved in mean accuracy from 54 percent before training to 86 percent after training, and mean fluency scores rose from 30 percent to 66 percent. Fourth-year medical students' mean accuracy scores moved from 58 percent to 85 percent and their fluency scores went from 33 percent to 68 percent. Emergency medicine residents improved from 76 percent to 90 percent in mean accuracy scores, and from 46 percent to 78 percent in fluency. Moreover, the results showed that improvements persisted for at least one year after training.

The Sensory Fidelity Principle has also been a hallmark of training for sports performance. Peter Fadde is a learning and expertise researcher who has been a strong advocate for recognition skills training that leverages videos of actual sport performance to provide high sensory fidelity in terms of visual cues. He describes a training program to aid baseball players in recognizing different types of pitches, thus improving their batting performance. Using a technique called video occlusion, baseball players are exposed to videos of baseball pitches and asked to identify the type of pitch being thrown. After the learner identifies the pitch type, they see the rest of the video, providing immediate feedback regarding the accuracy of the response. They begin with clips that end after 1/3 of ball flight and increase in difficulty by showing increasingly shorter video clips. The most difficult condition stops the video at the moment of release. Exposure to this type of recognition skills training resulted in significant improvements in batting average for college athletes (Burroughs, 1984; Fadde, 2006).

A recent research project explored an application of the Sensory Fidelity Principle in developing augmented reality-based refresher training for deployed combat medics called Trainer for Advanced Life Support in Austere Regions (TALSAR) (Militello et al., 2021). TALSAR is designed to run on smartphones and tablets, and focuses on patients and conditions that are not routine, but that military medics must be prepared to treat. For example, deployed medical personnel, who typically treat military-aged males, may be called on to treat pediatric patients from the local population. Although many medics receive pediatric life support training, they are

(a)   (b)   (c)

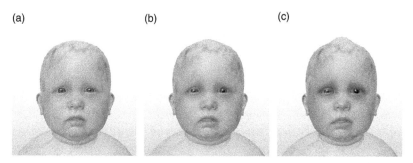

Figure 5.1 Increasing bulging fontanelle in a six-month-old infant with a head injury

rarely presented with opportunities to practice and refine these skills. One TALSAR scenario includes a six-month-old infant with a head injury. Examining an infant for evidence of head injury is different from examining an adult. One important cue to look for is bulging at the infant's soft spot where the bones of the skull have not completed development, called the fontanelle. Combat medics may not remember to examine the fontanelle, or they may be unsure what a healthy infant skull looks like compared to a child with a head injury. TALSAR uses dynamic visual representations of a bulging fontanelle as it develops over time in a virtual patient. The learner is able to walk around the virtual patient to view the fontanelle from different perspectives and compare the look of the fontanelle immediately following an injury to the look of the fontanelle as the infant's condition progresses. Figure 5.1 shows the progression of a bulging fontanelle.

5.1.4   Links to Macrocognition

The recognition-primed decision model (Klein et al., 1988) provides a theoretical rationale for the Sensory Fidelity Principle. Kahneman and Klein (2009) explain that the recognition-primed decision model implies two conditions are needed for recognition to develop. First, the environment must offer valid cues to the situation. Second, people must have the opportunity to learn the relevant cues. This includes adequate opportunity to practice the skill and receive accurate feedback. If we accept the premise that exposure to and the opportunity to learn valid cues are prerequisites for developing recognition skills "in the wild," then it follows that training intended to support skill development will benefit from these same conditions.

One benefit of leveraging the Sensory Fidelity Principle in designing recognition skills training is that it facilitates the development of experience-based intuitions. Sensory fidelity brings the training experience closer to real-world experience. Kahneman and Klein (2009) point out that people develop intuitions that guide their decision-making, sometimes referred to as heuristics. When these heuristics are based on flimsy evidence that is particularly salient, or that they have heard many times, they can lead to poor decision-making. Alternatively, intuitions and heuristics that are based on specific experiences that better reflect how cues occur in a particular domain are more trustworthy and can lead to better decision-making. By providing learners a base of realistic experiences, they are able to develop adaptive intuitions that lead to effective recognition skills. Conversely, training experiences with limited sensory fidelity can lead to negative learning, sometimes described as training scars or negative transfer. For example, the idea that video games can strengthen cognitive skills and improve performance on operational tasks has been popular for some decades; yet a recent meta-analysis failed to reveal compelling evidence to support this notion, and found that in some cases performance on real-world tasks got worse (Lintern & Boot, 2021; Lintern et al., 1997).

Another benefit of leveraging the Sensory Fidelity Principle is that training to support pattern recognition may well reduce cognitive load related to assessing routine aspects of the situation, freeing up cognitive capacity for sensemaking and problem-solving activities needed to manage uncertainty and interpret unexpected factors (Fadde, 2009; Kellman & Krasne, 2018). Experienced instructors provide anecdotal support for this concept. For example, when military personnel are learning to jump from aircraft, initially it takes all of their capacity to focus on pulling the parachute release cord at the right time. As they develop the perceptual skills to confidently recognize the time to pull the cord, they have more capacity to scan the terrain for obstacles, risks, and opportunities, along with coordinating with team members, thereby reducing uncertainty and updating their understanding of the situation as they approach the ground. In medicine, being able to efficiently interpret medical images gives rise to higher-order pattern recognition, such as recognizing abnormal patterns on a monitor, interpreting a large constellation of signs and symptoms to identify potential diagnoses, and dealing with atypical anatomy (Kellman & Krasne, 2018).

5.1.5 Summary and Discussion

The Sensory Fidelity Principle reflects the need to incorporate realistic cues into training to support perceptual skill development. Experts pick up on the critical cues and relevant patterns, often without awareness of what they are doing. These recognition skills allow them to make meaning and act quickly in complex situations. Beginners, in contrast, often struggle as they transition from formal education to on-the-job learning and performance – the July effect. Presenting realistic cues, especially in context, can help bridge this gap between declarative knowledge and the practical application of that knowledge in the form of recognition skills.

The recognition-primed decision model relies on two conditions for the development of recognition skills – the presence of cues and the opportunity to learn their importance and meaning. Augmented reality can present realistic sensory cues, but it can also offer features to support learners in understanding their importance, such as by drawing attention to important cues and helping learners create meaning. Using augmented reality to implement the Sensory Fidelity Principle can also help learners develop experienced-based intuitions that underlie decision-making in high-stress, time-pressured situations.

Sensory fidelity is important for training that focuses on improving perceptual skills. Augmented reality is particularly well suited to visual and auditory fidelity. Figure 5.2 depicts a series of frames used in a scenario that involves an infant that is rescued from the rubble after an explosion. These images contrast a typical infant posture with decerebrate and decorticate posturing. These postures are important indicators of brain damage and may not be obvious to those unaccustomed to treating children. The first panel shows a typical infant posture. The next shows decerebrate posturing; note how the baby's arms and legs are rigidly straight, toes are pointed, and head and neck are arched backward. The third panel shows decorticate posturing: the baby's arms are bent toward their body, but stiff. Their fists are clenched and held on their chest. Their legs are straight out. A child with brain damage may alternate between decerebrate and decorticate posturing. The virtual patient provides an opportunity to present realistic, dynamic sensory cues that are difficult to represent using other training modalities.

When viewed as a 3D virtual patient using augmented reality and combined with the presence or absence of the baby's cries, this creates a type of sensory fidelity that is difficult to obtain with other training modalities. The virtual patient can be combined with physical props such as a medical manikin to support tactile and functional fidelity. Even olfactory fidelity

(a)   (b)

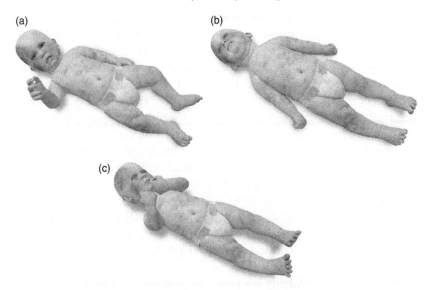

(c)

Figure 5.2 Example of a virtual patient contrasting typical infant posture with
decerebrate and decorticate posturing

can be integrated if scents represent an important perceptual cue for a specific task or domain. This can be accomplished using ubiquitous scents that are dispersed in the training space, or using a wearable device that transmits the scent closer to the learner. Using augmented reality, sensory cues can be depicted in different combinations in the context of different scenarios, and changes over time can be represented. The specific sensory cues and the contexts in which they are presented should be aligned with specific learning objectives. These sensory cues may be difficult to experience in other training settings.

It is worth noting that it is not always straightforward to specify valid cues or a valid environment. Determining which cues and environments are "realistic" is complicated by the fact that fidelity judgments are subjective; practitioners of different skill levels may have different perceptions of fidelity. For example, Singh and colleagues (2020) found that experienced pediatric anesthesiologists rated airway management training sessions as lower fidelity than medical fellows (e.g., physicians who have completed residency but are obtaining additional training in a specialty). The authors suggest that faculty are likely more aware of aspects of airway anatomy that are not well represented in manikins. In addition, in domains for which there is little direct feedback, even experienced practitioners have difficulty determining which cues and patterns are meaningful. For example, although economists spend considerable effort refining their ability to detect and interpret patterns in data, long-term forecasts of strategic and economic events are poor even by experts (Kahneman & Klein, 2009). The patterns are too complex, and the lack of direct feedback means such economic events cannot be forecast reliably. In other environments, observed patterns can be misleading. One well-known example is of the early twentieth-century physician who believed he could predict patients who would develop typhoid. He confirmed his intuitions by palpating the patients' tongues – and did not wash his hands in between. Whatever cues this unhygienic physician thought he identified as predicting typhoid were conflated with his spreading the infection with his own hands. The physician did not recognize the relationship between his dirty hands and typhoid infections in his patients (Hogarth, 2001, cited in Kahneman & Klein, 2009). Thus, it is critical that training designers identify and validate the critical cues they incorporate into training.

Although sensory fidelity is a powerful component of recognition skills training, it is just one component. Recognition skills training must also support mental model development so that cues and patterns of cues are accurately interpreted and lead to effective interventions. We discuss training principles to address mental model development in Chapter 6, Supporting Mental Model Construction.

5.1.6   Implications for Training Design

Realistic cues are needed to support the development of recognition skills. It is not enough to describe the realistic cues; rather, training designers must find ways to accurately represent them so learners can practice recognizing them. This often includes combining cues in meaningful ways. For example, specific visual cues may have different meanings depending on the accompanying audio cues. To balance the resource and labor costs of developing high-fidelity sensory cues, designers must determine which cues are most critical to depict realistically. This may include evaluating trade-offs. For example, in learning about airway injuries, fidelity in representing the patient's face and airway is more important than the patient's feet. Critical cues are driven by the learning objectives and goals of the training.

We recommend conducting formative tests with experienced practitioners to ensure that cues are represented adequately. Research has shown that medical residents and medical faculty rated fidelity differently, indicating that students may not recognize inaccuracies (Singh et al., 2020). Without proper testing, training can be rated as realistic by learners, but not actually prepare them for the real world. Such formative testing does not need to include extensive formal evaluations; even presenting the training scenarios to experts in an informal setting can help in identifying artificialities.

When thinking about sensory fidelity, there is a tendency to focus on visual cues. However, critical cues can be auditory, tactile, and even olfactory. Depending on the learning objectives, it may be important to engage a range of senses.

- ✔ Prioritize visual, auditory, tactile, and olfactory cues that are critical to achieving your learning objectives.
- ✔ Consider cue *combinations* that are important to represent.
- ✔ Incorporate sensory fidelity into short flashcard presentations to highlight important cues and cue combinations.
- ✔ Incorporate sensory fidelity into scenarios that unfold over time to highlight cues in context.
- ✔ Conduct formative tests with subject matter experts to ensure that cues are realistically represented.

5.2 Scaling Fidelity Principle

Scaling Fidelity Principle. Virtual props should be at a scale close to the real world.

5.2.1 What Do We Mean by Scaling Fidelity?

Scaling fidelity refers to how closely elements in the simulated environment align with the real world in terms of size and physical scale. Many training technologies involve interactions on a computer screen using virtual reality or a combination of text, video, and still images. While there is certainly value to this type of training, some learning objectives are best addressed by actually moving through the space as you would in the real world. This is particularly valuable when designing training in domains that require efficient movement through an environment.

Of the many types of fidelity to consider (e.g., sensory fidelity, task fidelity, psychological fidelity, cognitive fidelity, functional fidelity), the benefits of scaling fidelity become more practical than ever with augmented reality. Augmented reality provides an opportunity to project photorealistic props at scale onto the environment. A virtual patient can appear on an empty gurney; monitors can appear on the periphery as they would in a hospital room. Prior to augmented reality, training developers could choose between building a dedicated simulation facility with physical mani-kins and monitors, or foregoing scaling fidelity and presenting highly adaptable cases on a computer screen. Augmented reality allows for scaling fidelity *and* is highly adaptable, providing a platform in which the behavior and appearance of life-sized simulated props can be changed in real time from an instructor dashboard.

5.2.2   Why Does Scaling Fidelity Matter?

Skilled performers coordinate their movements with visual information in the environment (sometimes referred to as *visual kinesthesis*; Gibson, 1958). For example, in many health-care domains, patient assessment involves knowing where to look, how to position your body, how to attend to both the patient and to physical monitors, and how to implement medical interventions even when the room might be full of other people such as during a resuscitation or a surgical procedure. This may be particularly challenging in performing surgery on an infant, when space is at a premium and careful orchestration of movement is required. Having a virtual patient and monitors at scale allows trainees to practice these skills in a way that will more closely align with the real world. Physical therapists need to learn to scan the room for obstacles before helping a patient to walk. Emergency department physicians need to learn to conduct a thorough head-to-toe assessment, attend to monitors, and obtain information from allied health professionals and the patient's family members. Combat medics may need to learn to position themselves and patients in the constrained space of a helicopter and still allow freedom of movement to assess and treat the patients. Looking beyond health care, coordinating one's movements with the visual information in the environment is important in vehicle maintenance, piloting, firefighting, and many other domains. For all of these situations, scaling fidelity allows the learner to practice assessing and managing spatial relationships, body position, and environmental scanning. Scaling fidelity aids trainees in learning not just which cues to attend to, but also how to manipulate their bodies to perceive them.

Another benefit of scaling fidelity is that it more accurately simulates time constraints than some other training technologies. If you are interacting in a virtual world on a computer screen, you can do things in an instant. In the physical world, it actually takes time to walk around and maneuver life-sized objects. When the simulated world accurately reflects the scale of the real world, it can also realistically reflect the real world in time scale. Scaling fidelity also allows the training to better represent some real-world stressors. A difficult-to-move patient or difficult-to-access part can make a task more challenging, and when combined with time constraints and other stressors can offer an opportunity to practice under less-than-optimal but realistic conditions. Scaling fidelity also has the benefit of creating an engaging learning environment. Moving around the environment as you would in the real world creates a level of stimulation that is difficult to obtain when seated and viewing a computer screen.

5.2.3 Examples and Empirical Support

Scaling fidelity facilitates physical practice that is not possible with training technologies that are not to scale. Research suggests that there are important benefits of physical practice that are not generally achieved using mental practice alone (Driskell et al., 1994). This is not to malign the value of mental practice. Mental practice studies in which learners are encouraged to cognitively rehearse without overt physical movement have shown performance improvements in trombone playing (Ross, 1985), maze puzzle-solving (Sackett, 1934, 1935), basic venipuncture (Sanders et al., 2007), and many other domains. Augmented reality and other technologies have paved the way for applications that support mental practice in novel and engaging ways. For example, in some computer-based training applications, the learner has an avatar that moves through the environment and takes action. Advanced Research Associate's Virtual Heroes Combat Medic serious game is one well-known example (www.virtualheroes.com/content/combat-medic). The learner mentally rehearses by controlling and observing the avatars. Another approach is to use simple videos, so learners may observe others accomplishing a task, critique performance, and mentally rehearse how they would improve on what they observed (Dror, 2011). Mental practice has been shown to be a practical, low-cost way to provide important training benefits (Driskell et al., 1994).

Scaling fidelity, however, makes it possible to integrate this type of mental practice with physical practice in interesting ways – particularly for tasks that have strong assessment *and* action components as many high-stakes jobs do. A life-sized virtual patient requires learners to practice moving through the

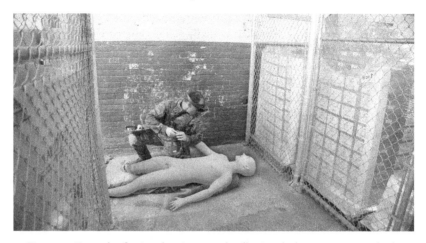

Figure 5.3 Example of a virtual patient at scale, allowing the learner to practice body
positioning as he assesses the patient

environment, positioning their bodies and perceiving the visual cues as they
would in the real world (Figure 5.3). There are important benefits to this.
Specifically, a meta-analysis of thirty-five studies describing training programs found that physical practice had a more robust effect than mental
practice; after just three weeks the benefits of mental practice had substan-
tially dissipated, but physical practice effects did not degrade at a similar rate
(Driskell et al., 1994). Combat medics often engage in training exercises to
practice treating patients in a variety of environments.

In a study of medical students learning to conduct a procedure called
cricothyrotomy, researchers found improved learning effects when physical
and mental practice were combined (Bathalon et al., 2005). A cricothyrotomy
is an emergency procedure used to institute an artificial airway when
ventilation and intubation are not possible. An incision is made in the
patient's neck through the cricothyroid membrane and a tube is placed in
the opening to allow the patient to breathe in spite of an airway obstruction.
The procedure is challenging because it must be done quickly, and incorrect
placement of the incision and tube can lead to negative patient outcomes.
Researchers from the University of Sherbrooke developed a training program
in which they used a cognitive task analysis technique to decompose the
cricothyrotomy task into eight steps. Second-year medical students were
trained in these eight steps. They observed a demonstration and then performed the procedure on a life-sized latex manikin. They received immediate
feedback on their performance, including guidance about proper handling of

instruments and proper body positioning. In the final five minutes of training, students were trained to use mental imagery: they were asked to "feel the operation rather than see it" (Bathalon et al., 2005, p. 329). They were asked to mentally practice the procedure using a pen as a knife and their fingers as a hemostat (a type of medical clamp). Researchers found that medical students who received both physical and mental practice scored better on accuracy of placement, required less time, and exhibited more fluid movements on an exam than those who received the standard Advanced Trauma Life Support training.

5.2.4   *Links to Macrocognition*

The Scaling Fidelity Principle aids learners in determining not just what to attend to, but also how to position their bodies so that they are able to see (and feel) specific cues. The data-frame model of sensemaking (Klein et al., 2006b) suggests that to create meaning, skilled performers must know what information to look for and how to find it. Critical cues are not static; by physically moving through the environment and interacting with props (virtual or physical) at scale, learners can practice the skills they need to identify and recognize critical cues in a dynamic environment. The data-frame model emphasizes that an individual's prior experience influences which cues are considered relevant and how they are interpreted. Scaling fidelity offers an opportunity for learners to practice physically investigating and making sense of cues in a simulated environment, helping them to build an experience base that will support sensemaking on the job.

5.2.5   *Summary and Discussion*

Scaling fidelity incorporates realistic physical movement into the training experience. This allows for an integration of mental and physical practice that is likely to lead to more robust and long-lasting learning than mental rehearsal alone. Providing an opportunity for learners to interact with life-sized objects in the environment helps learners bridge the gap between training and real-world practice. Using augmented reality to present objects to scale supports the development of recognition skills by allowing learners to practice the actual muscle movements associated with seeking out critical cues (e.g., move around the patient, raise one's head to look at a monitor, where to stand in a crowded room to assess a patient).

Scaling fidelity interacts with other types of fidelity and is subject to the same trade-off considerations (see Section 5.1 for a discussion of fidelity trade-offs). Furthermore, creating accurate scaling is not always straightforward. Physical manikins representing a portion of anatomy are commonly used in health-care training. For example, a manikin with only a head and neck may be used to practice treating airway injuries. These partial-body task trainers are a cost-effective way to provide the scaling fidelity needed to practice a specific set of skills. Even in this context, however, some researchers have highlighted that although the partial-body task trainer appears life-sized, many do not accurately reflect the size and location of human anatomy, potentially leading to negative task transfer and patient harm when faced with airway injuries in the real world (Cook et al., 2007; Jackson & Cook, 2007; Schebesta et al., 2012; Silsby et al., 2006; Timmermann, 2011; Winner & Millwater, 2019). Indeed, inaccurate anatomy is a risk with all non-human simulators including manikins and animals. The scaling fidelity required to practice body positioning may be sufficient using assets that fill the same general footprint as the real-world counterpart, but to practice assessment and intervention skills, the physical scale and position of anatomical features must be realistic as well.

5.2.6 Implications for Training Design

Scaling fidelity is particularly important for domains that require movement and spatial relationships. This could include positioning your body to see, hear, or feel important cues, as well as physical actions to manage the situation.

There is a trade-off associated with the device used to convey the virtual assets when addressing skills that require movement and spatial relationships. Headsets can be worn while moving around in a space for a hands-free experience that closely mimics movement in the real world, but headsets can be expensive and fragile. Using smartphones or tablets to convey the virtual content is less expensive, but the learner must carry the phone or tablet which adds a layer of artificiality to the movement and spatial relationships to be learned.

✔ Emphasize scaling fidelity for tasks that require movement and spatial relationships.
✔ Consider scaling at a gross level (i.e., is the virtual object life-sized?) and also at a more granular level (i.e., are the features of the virtual object to scale?).
✔ Consider the tradeoffs associated with different devices (augmented reality headset, smartphone, tablet, etc.) and how they support or hinder learning objectives related to movement and spatial relationships.

5.3   Assessment–Action Pairing Principle

Assessment–Action Pairing Principle. It is important to create a learning experience that allows the learner to both assess the situation and act.

5.3.1   What Do We Mean by Assessment–Action Pairing?

Including both assessing and acting in the training experience is an important type of realism for recognition skills training. For many complex tasks, there is an assessment component and an action component. Assessment is about sizing up the situation to determine what is going on. Acting includes any of a range of interventions or even a decision to continue to monitor the situation. These may sound like two distinct skills and are sometimes treated as distinct in training and evaluation. However, in reality the two skills are merged; assessment and action are inextricably linked. When we use the term assessment–action pairing, we are looking for training strategies that provide the learner an opportunity to learn and practice both assessment and action in the same learning experience. At a basic level, assessment–action pairing is about linking elements that may have been learned initially in a conceptual way. Learners may have read about specific cues and clusters of cues that suggest a certain condition, and also about what actions to take for specific conditions. Seeing and experiencing these *together* in a training environment can help the learner operationalize these concepts. However, there is also an integration component to assessment–action pairing. In the real world, people must often act before they have completed a thorough analysis; they must learn to determine when they have time to gather more information and when they must act. A combat medic, for example, may begin assessment, and quickly take actions to stabilize the patient, continuing to assess as the interventions are administered and the patient's condition changes. In fact, determining how quickly to act and what actions to take are a core component of assessment. Administering an intervention involves updating one's assessment based on the patient's reaction to the intervention, as well as changes in the patient's condition.

5.3.2   Why Does Assessment–Action Pairing Matter?

The concept of simplifying a complex task for training purposes as a way of building skill gradually or stepwise (sometimes referred to as "crawl, walk, run," or progressive difficulty) has taken many forms. The idea of separating training focused on assessment from training focused on action is intuitively appealing. Not only is it easier from a pragmatic perspective, the idea of having the learner focus on one skill at a time seems as if it would reduce the intrinsic load of trying to learn multiple things at the same time. Video-based part-task training approaches have been used effectively in certain tasks, notably sports such as rugby, tennis, and soccer (Engelbrecht et al., 2016; Farrow et al., 1998; Larkin et al., 2018; and Mann et al., 2007). Research suggests, however, that there may be important drawbacks to this part-task training approach (Wickens et al., 2013). Specifically, by pulling apart two tasks that are performed concurrently in the real world, learners may fail to learn the necessary attention management, coordination, perceptual, and psychomotor skills critical to skilled performance. Interestingly, a recent meta-analysis found that part-task training failed for tasks that are intended to be performed concurrently but was effective for tasks that are intended to be performed sequentially (Wickens et al., 2013). These findings support the value of pairing perceptual activities with physical actions.

Many training traditions emphasize the importance of assessment–action pairing. Military trainers often use the phrase "train like we fight," and sports coaches emphasize the importance of frequent scrimmaging. In addition to findings from scientific studies, many training traditions provide practical evidence of the value of creating learning experiences that allow the learner to practice skill integration.

5.3.3   Examples and Empirical Support

Most training that effectively incorporates assessment–action pairing is in the form of on-the-job training. However, important advancements allow this type of training to occur earlier in the training pipeline as more sophisticated, portable, and cost-effective simulation technologies become available. Modern simulation centers at large academic medical centers and medical schools include physical manikins that present increasingly realistic assessment cues. Manikins can bleed, breathe, and speak. The learner can place ports for intravenous fluids, do chest compressions, intubate, and practice many other medical interventions. These simulation centers provide a platform for creating challenging scenarios that provide practice at assessing, administering interventions, and reassessing as the patient's condition changes over time. The drawback is that these simulation centers are expensive to build, maintain, and run. As a result, they are not feasible for frequent, large-scale training. Each simulation session requires significant preparation and staff to run the actual simulation. Furthermore, some critical cues such as changes in skin tone, burns, and asymmetric rise and fall of the chest are difficult to present on a physical manikin.

Similarly, the military has a long tradition of live exercises that require participants to assess a dynamic situation, act, and reassess over time. More recently, they have invested in developing lower-cost, often screen-based simulations, sometimes called serious games, that incorporate this Assessment–Action Pairing Principle to augment live training exercises. For example, the Stratagems trainer developed by Stottler-Henke Associates and ShadowBox, LLC is a game-based trainer designed to support combat search and rescue pilots in quickly assessing a dynamic situation, prioritizing information needs, and acting (Newsome et al., 2020). This trainer runs on a desktop computer and leverages an existing first-person perspective helicopter flight game. The research team developed training scenarios based on real-life incidents described by experienced pilots and implemented them in the game software. As the scenario unfolds, the learner receives audio updates via simulated radio communications. At key points, game play is paused, and learners are presented with a multiple-choice probe in which they must rank information needs, assess risk (Figure 5.4), or prioritize actions (Figure 5.5). The path of the game is influenced by the actions they choose. They may receive access to information they evaluate as high priority and be denied information they rate as low priority. The likelihood of crashing or being shot down varies based on risk ratings and actions selected. After completing the scenario, pilots are presented with their own responses to each probe as well as responses of a panel of experienced pilots to encourage reflection. The intent of this serious game is to give pilots an opportunity to anticipate challenging situations they are likely to encounter and to mentally practice accurately assessing the situation and taking appropriate actions – all in a low-cost and safe environment (Newsome et al., 2020).

Augmented reality offers interesting opportunities to incorporate the assessment–action pairing in combat medic training. Unveil and North American Rescue have teamed to develop this type of assessment–action pairing training in the Virtual Patient Immersive Trainer^{TM} for use in training tactical combat casualty care to combat medics (https://unveilsystems.com). Figure 5.6 shows how the virtual patient and physical manikin are used together. Frame A depicts the view of the virtual patient as seen by the learner through the augmented reality headset (in this case, Microsoft's HoloLens headset). Although difficult to see in black and white, the virtual patient provides the detail needed for the learner to conduct a thorough assessment, examining the wounds, watching the rise and fall of the patient's chest, and noting facial expressions. Frame B shows the learner treating the patient by placing a chest seal over the wound on the physical

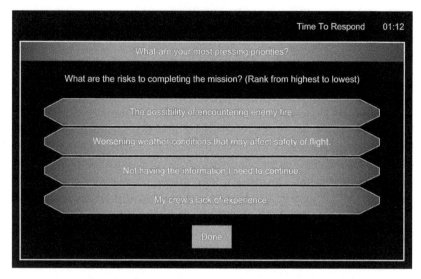

Figure 5.4 Example of probe asking the learner to assess risks in the Stratagems trainer

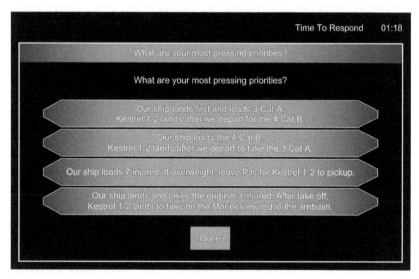

Figure 5.5 Example of probe asking the learner to prioritize actions in the Stratagems trainer

(a)   (b)

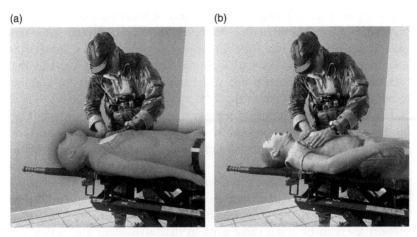

Figure 5.6 Example of assessment–action pairing as the learner assesses dynamic photorealistic cues on the virtual patient and practices treating the physical manikin using real-world instruments

manikin. Use of a manikin allows learners to use actual instruments and medical supplies as they would in the real world, and the instructor can easily change the look of the virtual patient based on learner performance. For example, if a tourniquet was not tightened enough, the learner may see continued bleeding and observe no change in skin tone, indicating that the intervention was not effective. Conversely, if the tourniquet is placed correctly, the learner would see improvements in skin tone and no new bleeding.

5.3.4 Links to Macrocognition

The recognition primed decision model emphasizes that skilled performers rapidly size up a situation and know what to do (Klein et al., 1988). Knowing what to do might include seeking more information to better understand the situation or taking action to influence the situation. Because of the tight coupling between assessment and action, learning environments that allow learners to practice these skills together are critical to supporting skilled performance, particularly in domains characterized by time pressure and rapidly changing situations such as combat medicine. Separating assessment from action in training may seem appealing from a pragmatic perspective. It is easy to practice assessment skills by presenting videos and images to large groups in a classroom setting. Practice acting may happen more effectively in the context of individual or small-group training in a simulation facility. However, this approach may leave skill gaps as learners will not have an opportunity to practice integrating assessment and action. Part-task training may be effective for tasks that typically occur in sequence but will likely be insufficient for training recognition skills (Wickens et al., 2013).

This importance of linking assessments and action also appears in Don Norman's (1986) writing on cognitive engineering. Norman's focus is on user-interface design rather than training, but the underlying concept is the same. He cautions against designing technologies that make it difficult for the user to execute an action based on their understanding of the situation (referred to as the *Gulf of Execution*) or to evaluate the outcomes of their actions (referred to as the *Gulf of Evaluation*). Well-designed interfaces support users in bridging these gaps so that assessment and action can happen seamlessly without interference by the technology.

5.3.5 Summary and Discussion

Assessment–action pairing is a reality during on-the-job performance, especially for highly dynamic, time-pressured tasks. The notion that assessment and action are linked appears in macrocognitive (Klein et al., 1988) and cognitive engineering models (Norman, 1986). The Assessment–Action Pairing Principle advocates for creating training that allows learners to practice not just assessment and action skills in isolation, but also integrates these skills in the context of challenging scenarios. This is particularly important for recognition skills training because assessing and acting happen iteratively, and sometimes concurrently. Actions are occasionally taken as part of assessment to gather more information and reduce uncertainty. Sometimes actions have unexpected outcomes, changing one's understanding of the situation in important ways. Assessment–action pairing provides an opportunity to experience these patterns and interdependencies, strengthening the trainees' sensemaking skills.

There are many strategies for assessment–action pairing. Training may focus on mental practice by presenting learners with a challenging situation and encouraging them to assess the situation and describe the actions they would take. Alternatively, training may incorporate sensory cues to support assessment, and physical assets to support action practice.

Creating a training experience that incorporates both assessment and action is not straightforward. Often the sensory and scaling fidelity required for realistic assessment is most easily created in a virtual medium;

whereas the physical components such as tools and equipment needed to practice acting are best represented with physical props. Physical props may be needed to help learners refine physical dexterity and coordination skills. Augmented reality technologies provide an opportunity to integrate virtual assets with physical assets to achieve training that supports practice at both assessing and acting in the context of challenging scenarios.

5.3.6 Implications for Training Design

The blended virtual and physical world provides interesting opportunities for a learning experience that includes both assessing a situation and acting. In more sophisticated training applications, the software that drives the virtual assets can be paired with the software that controls the physical assets to create an integrated learning experience. As the learner takes actions with and on the physical assets, the appearance of the virtual assets can respond. In this way, the learner obtains feedback from their actions just as they would in the real world.

For less technologically sophisticated training applications, learners can conduct an assessment in the blended virtual–physical world and describe the actions they would take. This type of mental rehearsal has been shown to have training benefits. In many contexts, mental rehearsal may be a useful but not final step in the learning process.

As with other types of fidelity, determining which assessment and actions to emphasize in training should be guided by specific learning objectives.

✔ Use learning objectives to guide the design of important assessment–action pairs.
✔ Link assessment and action in training to avoid training scars.
✔ Integrate virtual assets with physical props so interactions with physical props affect how the virtual ones are represented, where possible.
✔ When integrating virtual and physical assets is not feasible, consider exercises in which learners assess virtual content, and then mentally rehearse appropriate actions by describing them.

CHAPTER 6

Supporting Mental Model Construction

"Mental model" is a term used to describe the internal representations humans create to guide interactions in the world. Mental models organize a person's understanding of concepts, events, processes, or systems (Klein & Hoffman, 2008). The goal of training is to create rich mental models that live in learners' long-term memories so they can be activated during real-world task performance (Fiore et al., 2003).

Part of acquiring expertise is developing robust experience-based mental models relevant to a specific work context. Novices often rely on superficial or sometimes even flawed mental models based on classroom knowledge and limited experience. As novices practice applying their mental models in a variety of circumstances, they are able to elaborate on the models, making them more complete and robust. Experts have rich mental models that allow them to make decisions and act in a broader range of contexts than novices.

We highlight two design principles focused on supporting learners in developing accurate and robust mental models. The Mental Model Articulation Principle emphasizes building training experiences that encourage learners to verbalize aspects of their mental models. The Many Variations Principle highlights the value of providing learners with a range of experiences with the intent of expanding their mental models to support performance in diverse conditions.

6.1 Mental Model Articulation Principle

Mental Model Articulation Principle. Training techniques that require the learner to articulate what they are noticing, how they are assessing the situation, and predictions about how the situation will evolve aid the learner in developing coherent mental models.

6.1.1 What Do We Mean by Mental Model Articulation?

We use the term mental model articulation to refer to techniques that encourage learners to construct and describe aspects of their thinking. Mental models are internal, experience-based structures that guide how people interpret a situation and act. They reflect an individual's understanding of what is going on and why something is happening. Mental models allow people to predict what will happen when they perform certain actions. Sometimes described as the internal representation of how things work, mental models may include structural and functional relationships, dependencies, and causal relationships between concepts, events, and actions. There is some controversy regarding whether people can articulate mental models; some suggest that this is deep tacit knowledge that cannot be described (Polanyi, 1966; Rouse & Morris, 1986). We are not concerned with the theoretical argument regarding whether people articulate mental models, or express simplified representations of a much more complex and richer aspect of expertise. Rather, our focus is on asking learners to articulate their own assessments and predictions, thereby encouraging them to actively test existing mental models and form new ones. By asking learners to articulate aspects of their own mental models, training provides a platform for self-reflection and comparison. The learner can consider whether the aspects of the mental model articulated remained useful as the training scenario unfolded. Instructors can better see flaws in mental models to tailor feedback. In some training settings, learners may have an opportunity to compare their understanding of the situation and predictions to that of peers and experts.

6.1.2 Why Is Mental Model Articulation Important?

Mental models guide how humans interpret and behave in all aspects of their lives. Flawed mental models can lead to errors. For example, drivers maintain a mental model about the effects of certain road conditions on the behavior of their vehicles. When driving on a wet or icy road, people generally expect that their cars will need longer to stop when they depress the brake pedal. For drivers of cars that were manufactured before the 1990s, mental models likely also include an understanding that if you hit the brake pedal too hard and too fast, the car might skid and therefore pumping the brake rather than applying steady pressure is the most effective strategy for slowing or stopping the car in certain conditions. However, cars manufactured after 2004 in the United States include anti-lock braking technology that eliminates the need to pump the brakes manually. Furthermore, the sensory feedback from the anti-lock brakes is quite different from traditional brakes. If one is driving a car with anti-lock brakes and operating with a flawed mental model based on outdated technology, the reaction of the anti-lock brakes is likely to be startling, making it more difficult for the driver to anticipate how the car will behave on slippery roads. After experiencing anti-lock brakes on a slick roadway, drivers are likely to expand their mental model to include a distinction between cars with and without anti-lock brakes.

This simple driving example extends to recognition skills in high-stakes, dynamic domains that are the focus of this handbook. Mental models inform timely assessment and treatment decisions of experienced combat medics; guide pilots in managing aircraft during both routine and non-routine situations; and support emergency department physicians in creating differential diagnoses and determining treatments and disposition for their patients. Without robust mental models, people tend to fall back on rote procedures that may not be adequate. Supporting learners in developing robust mental models allows them to perform smoothly and effectively during routine operations, and also increases the likelihood that they will be able to make intelligent and logical adaptations when confronted with novel conditions.

6.1.3   Examples and Empirical Support

Perhaps the most well-known application of the Mental Model Articulation Principle is the use of self-explanation advocated by Chi and colleagues (Chi et al., 1989). Self-explanation has been incorporated into formal education environments from elementary students to college students learning cognitively challenging concepts and procedures in topics such as chemistry, physics, mathematics, reading comprehension, and computer programming (Wylie & Chi, 2014). Many of these training applications leverage multimedia strategies incorporating text, diagrams, and simulations. Learners are asked to "self-explain," or describe their own understanding, with the intent of encouraging students to link information presented in different media (e.g., link textual description to spatial representations in a figure), form inferences, and map the inferences onto their existing mental models. Importantly, they are encouraged to note possible connections and formulate hypotheses rather than simply summarizing what they have read. Self-explaining supports students in identifying discrepancies and then expanding and adjusting their mental models as needed. Notably, self-explaining was found to have learning benefits even without an instructor to provide feedback (Schworm & Renkl, 2006).

Self-explaining initially took the form of open-ended prompts that encouraged students to make connections between what they had already learned and newly presented information (Chi et al., 1989; 1994), and has since been expanded to include focused, scaffolded, resource-based, and menu-based queries (Wylie & Chi, 2014). Concept mapping (Novak & Gowin, 1984), where students diagram concepts and relationships between them, is another form of self-explanation. Diagrams have been found to improve mental models in learners, likely due to increased elaboration of the material (Fiore et al., 2003).

Another interesting approach to the Mental Model Articulation Principle was implemented in a critical thinking course developed for the US Army Command and General Staff College (Cohen et al., 2000). This technique moves beyond the training of general concepts and procedures to training critical thinking and decision-making on the battlefield. The course included exercises in which learners received a text-based scenario including a plan of attack, and then constructed a diagram of the scenario articulating key components of their mental model of the situation and plan. In this case, the mental model articulation strategy included prompts to describe the mission from multiple perspectives (e.g., your own, your company's, and adjacent company's), the commander's intent, and the concept of operations. After constructing the diagram, learners were asked to identify gaps (Is important information missing from your mental model?), conflicts (Do different information sources, tasks, and/or purposes conflict?), and unreliable assumptions (Do important conclusions or plans depend on untested assumptions?). Learners were then presented with a new variant of the plan, drew a mental model diagram, and critiqued again. One objective of this approach was to help learners recognize common weaknesses in battle planning mental models (e.g., gaps, conflicts, and unreliable assumptions). An evaluation study found that this type of training had a positive effect on critical thinking processes and decisions. With regard to critical thinking, training led to more frequent use of commander's intent and articulation of more assumptions in battle plans. With regard to decisions, learners significantly increased their use of key tactical elements available (e.g., fires, ground attack, using high ground to defend important terrain features) and increased their use of combinations of those tactical elements. The mental model articulation and refinement exercises were one component of a larger training program, so although these empirical findings are promising, they cannot be attributed to mental model articulation alone.

ShadowBox training is yet another approach (Klein & Borders, 2016), combining mental model articulation with reflection exercises to amplify learning (see Section 7.2). In a series of studies of training designed to support US Marine Corps personnel in effectively managing military-civilian interpersonal encounters, researchers presented learners with text-based scenarios. At key points in each scenario, learners encountered question probes that required them to commit to an assessment, a prioritization, or an action by ranking a set of options, and to provide a rationale for their choice. After providing responses, they were presented with the ratings and rationales provided by a panel of experts and asked to reflect on and write down lessons learned and insights gained by the comparison. In one study, learners received a paper-based training module, while in another study learners received a virtual training module via an Android tablet. In the first study, those who received training showed a 28 percent improvement in performance (in terms of match to experts) as compared to the control group who did not receive ShadowBox training; and in the second study, learners exposed to ShadowBox training improved by 21 percent.

Another recent research project evaluated a training application for medical students that queried participants at key points during training scenarios (Hernandez, 2021). One group of medical students was presented with a series of challenging scenarios. Mental model articulation prompts encouraged them to report cues they were attending to, as well as their evolving assessment at key points in each scenario. They were exposed to an expert model at each of these decision points, in the form of an audio recording of an experienced physician describing his understanding of the situation. A second group was presented with the same scenarios, but not prompted to articulate aspects of their mental models and were not exposed to the expert model. Both groups received didactic training. Hernandez (2021) found that medical students asked to respond to mental model prompts and exposed to the expert model during training scenarios were better able to identify critical cues than medical students who experienced the same scenarios without the probes and expert model. Interestingly, there was no difference in correct diagnoses across groups for two of the three training scenarios.

Augmented reality provides a platform for incorporating self-explanation in more immersive ways. For example, augmented reality-based training might include an avatar that represents a colleague or supervisor who may

Figure 6.1 Augmented reality-based avatar asking questions to probe a learner's mental model

ask questions in the context of a training scenario (Figure 6.1). An avatar colleague might ask questions such as: What do you think is going on? What should we do next? What do you think is the most likely outcome? These queries might appear at key points in the scenario to encourage certain inferences, and to aid the learner in identifying flaws in thinking as the situation unfolds. Maintaining immersion in the scenario in this way may provide more a compelling learning experience.

6.1.4 Links to Macrocognition

People form, adapt, and expand mental models through experience. Much of traditional classroom-based curricula support this process. Elementary school students learn related mathematical concepts in close succession. Students learn how to add, then subtract; how to multiply, then divide. Students learn how to create simple sentences, then more complex ones. Before students learn how to combine chemical elements, they first learn about atoms and subatomic particles. With experience, mental models transform in important ways by becoming more elaborate to include new concepts and relationships (Seel & Dinter, 1995).

With regard to recognition skills, mental models underlie recognition primed decision-making and sensemaking. The types of rapid assessments and actions that we observe with expert firefighters, medics, nurses, and pilots are based on sophisticated mental models. Fiore and colleagues (2003) described the structure of mental models as subsets of knowledge structures that are task specific and integrated. If training is effective, mental models learned in training will be activated at appropriate times on the job. However, this happens only if one is engaged in learning and actively constructing, refining, and expanding mental models during the training experience. Otherwise, mental models developed during training are brittle, activated only when conditions closely match the training conditions. The Mental Model Articulation Principle is intended to create a training environment that encourages active mental model formation.

6.1.5   Summary and Discussion

The Mental Model Articulation Principle advocates for creating a training experience that encourages learners to articulate aspects of their mental models. Augmented reality can prompt learners to articulate their mental models in several ways. A virtual avatar may pose as a colleague asking the learner questions. Written prompts may be used to query learners. Learners may articulate responses that make visible components of their mental models using free-text, free-speech, or multiple choice. Having learners reflect on their mental models encourages mental model construction and reveals flaws and gaps in their understanding. The strategy of self-explaining has been used successfully in training complex concepts and procedures in subjects such as physics and chemistry. Similar types of probes have been embedded in scenarios for training more dynamic, high-stakes tasks such as managing civilian–military interactions and emergency medicine. Robust mental models are the foundation of expert perform-ance. Mental models help practitioners recognize important cues, create meanings from those cues, and develop expectancies about how a situation is likely to evolve. When unexpected events arise, robust mental models help practitioners adapt.

One challenge for scenario-based training is that interrupting the scenario with mental model articulation prompts breaks the flow and may reduce the learner's sense of immersion. This may be a reasonable trade-off for certain training goals. For example, if the goal is to provide refresher training for proficient practitioners, training that encourages learners to pause, articulate aspects of their mental models, and reflect may be an important complement to time-pressured, on-the-job experiences. On the other hand, if the goal is to help those new to the job practice smooth, time-pressured performance in preparation for real-world challenges, pausing the scenario may work against training goals. The loss of immersion may prevent learners from practicing the very skills needed to achieve training goals.

For training in which immersion is considered critical, the use of avatars to represent colleagues or supervisors who ask questions at key points in the scenario is one strategy for encouraging mental model articulation while maintaining immersion in the training scenario. Augmented reality can also be used to incorporate hints, procedures, and conceptual links to aid learners in extending existing mental models in the context of challenging training scenarios.

6.1.6 Implications for Training Design

When incorporating the Mental Model Articulation Principle, training designers must determine which mental model components are needed to support the learning objectives, design elements to elicit the learner's mental model, and create a method for presenting the expert mental model.

To determine which mental model components are needed, consider the learning objectives and the domain. For example, in health-care domains, learners may be asked to articulate an assessment or differential diagnosis, treatment options, and likely disposition of the patient (i.e., will the patient go home or be admitted to the hospital). For combat search and rescue pilots, mental model components might include prioritized risks, planned actions, and contingencies. These mental model components will guide the design of mental model probes.

To develop an expert mental model that will inform feedback during training, training designers should consult with multiple experts. In dynamic, high-stakes domains, there is often more than one right answer. Representing multiple perspectives about how to handle a challenging situation can help learners appreciate complexity and develop adaptive strategies. The expert model should include preferred responses as well as the experts' rationale.

It is important to pilot the mental model probes and expert model feedback with a sample group of target users. To designers, the intent of the probes and the expert model feedback may be very clear, but learners may interpret them differently.

> ✔ Use learning objectives to determine what probes will elicit relevant components of the learners' mental models.
> ✔ Consult multiple experts when developing the expert model that will drive feedback to learners.
> ✔ Conduct formative testing of the mental model probes and the expert model feedback mechanism with a group of target users.

6.2   Many Variations Principle

Many Variations Principle. Training techniques that expose the learner to many variations with different levels of difficulty support development of robust mental models.

6.2.1   What Do We Mean by Many Variations?

The Many Variations Principle highlights the importance of exposing learners to the types of variation they will encounter in the real world. A mental model built on application of standard operating procedures in an idealized setting may be a useful starting place, but this type of mental model is not sufficient for proficient performance on the job. Rather, exposing learners to a range of scenarios that include realistic variations in presentation of cues, application of procedures, and plausible outcomes creates an opportunity to develop robust mental models that will generalize to a broader range of circumstances on the job.

We see this approach in traditional classroom education. In math class, teachers begin by presenting basic equations to be solved, then bury the mathematical principles into the dreaded "word problems," where students must pick out the pertinent information and determine the appropriate mathematical principles to apply. Word problems help students contextualize the principles being taught in a variety of ways.

In complex domains such as medicine, presenting a variety of training scenarios becomes even more important to help learners contextualize knowledge in novel situations. For example, signs or symptoms may appear differently depending on a patient's sex or age. Signs of a heart attack can vary between men and women, and children's bodies are more adept at hiding early signs of serious conditions such as sepsis, which can delay diagnosis. To develop expertise, learners must experience enough variation in training scenarios to recognize the critical constraints that underlie the problem space or skill they are learning (Hoffman et al., 2013; Kellman & Krasne, 2018; Ward et al., 2018).

6.2.2 Why Are Many Variations Important?

The real world is complex. Developing robust mental models that will be effective in high-stakes, unpredictable, and dynamic environments requires practice designed to support mental model elaboration. A common assumption about how people learn is that the mind is a container. If you fill it up with relevant facts, the person will be able to retrieve those facts when needed. However, research has shown that this "mind as container" metaphor is too simplistic and breaks down when learners move out of a classroom environment where the goal is to answer questions correctly on a test, and into the world where they must apply the knowledge in novel ways. Kellman and Krasne (2018) point out that traditional medical education adopted this mind as a container metaphor, focusing on teaching declarative and procedural knowledge. However, experience tells us that resident physicians fresh from medical school often miss the critical patterns in real life, failing to apply correct procedures or taking too long to make decisions (Cohen et al., 2013). This is the "July effect" discussed in Section 5.1 on Sensory Fidelity. It is when resident physicians begin working in hospital settings that they are exposed to the real-world variations required to create robust mental models needed to guide skilled performance. To ease the transition from learning to application, the Many Variations Principle encourages training designers to help learners practice applying their mental models to diverse and realistic training scenarios.

6.2.3 Examples and Empirical Support

Robert Patterson and colleagues have created a strategy for training intuitive decision-making that leverages the Many Variations Principle (Patterson et al., 2010). They created a simulation environment to test training techniques intended to support intuitive decision-making skills for the types of pattern recognition skills used in combat search and rescue. In the simulator, participants viewed vehicles positioned on the ground from an aerial view as if from an aircraft. The training included variations in the dynamic environment designed to induce implicit learning of dynamic patterns and features – components of mental models that are notoriously difficult to articulate. One example of a variation in the dynamic environment included trucks that appeared in different locations and at different times. Variations were generated using an algorithm that informed the number, type, and location of objects in the environment that participants encountered so there was an underlying logic to the behavior of objects. Over a twenty-seven-minute training period, participants were exposed to eighteen vehicle sequences. After completing the training, participants were presented with test trials and asked to distinguish those that showed vehicles taking new paths generated by the same algorithm from vehicles taking random paths.

Investigators explored different training strategies in this context. One condition of particular interest was the passive training condition. Participants who received passive training were not instructed to learn anything, were not told where to direct their attention, did not receive feedback, and were not told that they would be tested at a later point in time. The rationale was that this is how much learning happens on the job in the real world; people experience many variations but get little overt training or feedback about how to learn from these experiences. Even in this passive training condition participants were able to distinguish new paths generated by the algorithm from random paths significantly better than a no-training group. Furthermore, there was no significant difference in performance between those in the passive training condition and those who were explicitly told to memorize object paths after viewing them and received feedback on their responses during training. Although this training focused on a relatively narrow type of recognition skill, these findings support the idea that simple exposure to many variations helps learners begin to recognize patterns and relationships that are critical to mental model development and skilled performance. This finding is supported anecdotally by physicians who describe how residents must see series of rashes with the same etiology before they can pick out the common features or characteristics of a particular condition. Further, learners must see multiple examples of how that rash may evolve to improve their ability to anticipate the patient's future condition.

Fadde (2007) also advocates for expanding the number and type of situations trainees experience in creating recognition skills training. He discusses examples from several domains including truck driving, radiology, and law enforcement. He suggests that there may be value in creating shorter "video flashcards" (rather than full-scale scenarios) to make exposure to many situations feasible. Another strategy is to vary the point at which learners engage with the training task. Musicians sometimes practice by varying the starting point, starting to play in the middle of a piece of music. This requires learners to adapt when cues are presented out of order and to be prepared to play fluidly in unanticipated situations. Fadde notes that sports and music have a "culture of practice" (MacMahon et al., 2007) that promotes exposure to many variations as part of deliberate practice (Ericsson et al., 1993) and acquisition of recognition skills that other domains would do well to imitate.

Augmented reality can be used to support the Many Variations Principle by presenting a variety of realistic scenarios. Digital assets allow for rapidly shifting from one patient presentation to another at the click of a button. A trainer can present the same patient with a single gunshot wound, multiple gunshot wounds, a clean exit wound, no exit wound, and many other variations in rapid succession. As an example, Figure 6.2 shows many variations of gunshot wounds to the arm. It may take weeks or years to see these various injuries on the job, and obtain the skills needed to quickly assess and treat. A trainer that presents these many variations may support learners in building and extending mental models as they note important differences and similarities across the different gunshot wounds. Augmented reality also allows for photorealistic presentation of rare and potentially dangerous variations in the safety of a simulation. Notably, some researchers suggest that

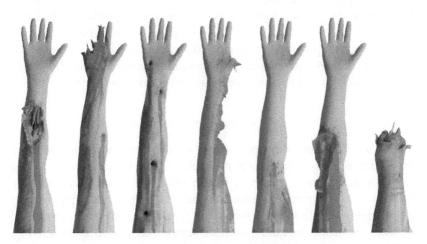

Figure 6.2 Many variations of a gunshot wound to an arm

exposure to many variations in training may result in slower learning of initial skills and more errors during training, but will lead to more robust mental models that are easier to translate to the real world (Healy, 2007; Keith & Frese, 2008). The "video flashcards" that Fadde suggested can also be implemented using augmented reality; brief vignettes can be created and shown in quick succession using augmented reality technology. This may be particularly useful in domains for which it is difficult to obtain videos of actual performance.

6.2.4   Links to Macrocognition

The recognition-primed decision model states that when experts encounter a situation, they pick up on key features of the situation and determine whether it is similar to something they have experienced before. If the situation is familiar, an expert is able to generate expectations about how the situation is likely to unfold, seek out key information while disregarding extraneous details, and determine reasonable goals and actions. Mental models underlie these activities. Experts learn to recognize situations based on past experiences and active reflection on those experiences. Their sophisticated mental models allow them to recognize when underlying patterns are similar, even if surface details vary dramatically. They can recognize when situations are abnormal, and they can apply their existing knowledge and skills in new ways. Some researchers argue that the defining feature of expertise is this ability to apply knowledge in novel situations, known as *adaptive skill* (Ward et al., 2018). The Many Variations Principle is intended to provide learners one of the critical building blocks of recognition skills – a case base of varied experiences. Conversely, if learners are provided an opportunity to practice skills in the context of a very limited number of scenarios or conditions, the resulting mental models will be very specific and may lead to misconceptions and performance deficits.

6.2.5   Summary and Discussion

The Many Variations Principle is based on the idea that learners must be exposed to a range of experiences to develop robust mental models needed to adapt and perform effectively in dynamic, high-stakes jobs. Exposing learners to a wide variety of situations helps them practice applying their knowledge and skills in novel ways. This type of training has been applied in many domains, including combat search and rescue, truck driving, radiology, law enforcement, sports, and music. Note that the Many

Variations Principle is related to but different from the Perturbation Principle described in Chapter 4 on Scenario Building. The Many Variations Principle emphasizes that learners need exposure to many variations to develop robust mental models. For medics this might include presentation of the same type of injury in many different patients; for soccer goalies, this might include exposure to penalty shots taken by many different players. The Perturbation Principle focuses on exposure to unexpected events or roadblocks, such as a technology breakdown, a lack of resources, or a disruption in communication with team members with the intent of providing practice at adapting to manage the unexpected.

Providing students with the opportunity to apply their knowledge in a wide variety of situations can help them develop an experience base that encourages the development of more robust mental models. This experience base also helps students learn about critical cues and develop expectancies when they encounter similar situations in the real world. In terms of building recognition skills, the Many Variations Principle supports all three components (knowing what to attend to, creating meaning, and evaluating) by providing opportunities for students to practice in a variety of scenarios.

Augmented reality may facilitate the creation of many variations in training scenarios. Digital assets can be adapted and combined in a range of ways, creating efficiency in developing scenarios with both minor and major variations. Scenarios and patient presentations can be rapidly changed to provide a flashcard-type presentation of many variations in relatively rapid succession. Students can engage with scenarios as they begin, in the middle, or near the end to practice assessing, acting, and adapting in a variety of ways within the same scenario.

6.2.6 Implications for Training Design

Creating many variations of training scenarios can be resource intensive. To maintain an appropriate scope of work, it is important to focus on the types of variations that are meaningful in the context of the training goals and learning objectives. Cognitive task analysis can provide insight into the skills experts develop for the task, variations that are important to recognize, and variations that are difficult to distinguish.

For the learner, feedback is a critical component in figuring out how the variations differ and the implications of those variations. Training designers should incorporate methods for providing feedback to learners that focus on important discriminations between variations and recognizing themes among groups of variations. Beginners tend to focus on differences in surface features, but feedback can help them learn to focus on differences in structural or conceptual features as well.

✔ Focus on creating meaningful variations based on learning objectives and training goals.
✔ Use the expert model to help identify meaningful variations.
✔ Highlight important discriminations between variations during feedback and debriefing.

CHAPTER 7

Scaffolding and Reflection

Skilled instructors develop creative strategies for supporting learners (scaffolding) and for facilitating reflection. While most instructors recognize the value of tailoring instruction to the learner's needs, strategies and skills for supporting learning vary widely across instructors. In this chapter, we consider advances made in developing technologies to either support skilled instructors or provide stand-alone instruction without the presence of an instructor. We summarize research on scaffolding and reflection that is particularly relevant to developing recognition skills in dynamic, high-stakes domains, and explore two principles aimed at tailoring training to the needs of users. The Scaffolding Principle and the Reflection Principle advocate for training that considers the skill level of the learner, as well as the training environment and culture. Augmented reality can be used to implement these principles by providing a platform for visual hints, including pointers, highlighting, and animations depicting relationships that may be difficult to visualize in the real world.

7.1 Scaffolding Principle

Scaffolding Principle. Student-centered learning support can be used to promote recognition skill development at different skill levels.

7.1.1 What Do We Mean by Scaffolding?

Scaffolding is an instructional technique that is designed to move learners progressively toward stronger understanding and greater independence (Wilson & Devereux, 2014). Like a building scaffold, the purpose of instructional scaffolding is to provide support to learners as they construct their own knowledge, helping learners work through difficult concepts until they are able to understand the material on their own. This idea of scaffolding is strongly related to adaptive training as the kind and degree of support required by a learner will necessarily evolve with time and increasing expertise.

In the context of training, scaffolding often takes the form of hints and prompts that help a learner work through a task or scenario that is beyond their current skill level. These can take many forms, from abstract to concrete. They can be provided as visual cues and pointers, animations, or spoken/text-based messages. Augmented reality considerably expands the types of hints that may be given. The concept of scaffolding has its roots in the notion of placing learners in the zone of proximal development (Vygotsky, 1978) by creating a high-challenge, high-support experience (Mariani, 1997). What constitutes a high-challenge, high-support experience will vary depending on the skill level of the learner. For a novice, this might include a guided walkthrough of a challenging procedure. For a mid-level learner, it might include doing a similar procedure in a scenario that includes additional complexities or interruptions, with hints and coaching or other interventions to prevent the learner from going too far off-track. By hints, we mean prompts provided to help the student's understanding of the situation and determine actions to take. Coaching is similar to hints but could be more directed and specific (i.e., an explicit instruction to do something a certain way).

Hints and coaching are typically provided during a scenario. In some instances, if a learner is way off track and seems unlikely to recover, the scenario may be briefly paused to give learners a chance to refocus or to relieve time pressure. Learners may also be permitted to make some errors but receive immediate corrective feedback so they may complete the training experience. For a skilled learner, training might include a challenging scenario with no scaffolding support during the exercise, followed by targeted feedback during a debrief session at the end. Although there has been some controversy, many advocate for allowing advanced learners to fail during training so that learners can experience highly impactful learning experiences that would not be safe in the real world (Klasen & Lingard, 2019). Due to the potential psychological impact of failures, training developers must carefully consider whether the benefits outweigh the potential distress and discouragement a learner may experience. For example, an important failure in health care is having a patient die. Experiencing the death of a patient in a simulation may support important learning objectives such as understanding how hesitating to act when faced with a hemorrhage injury can lead to death in minutes, but may have little relevance for some other learning objectives.

A core tenet of scaffolding is that the learning experience should be beyond the learner's current capabilities: Instruction is only useful when it moves ahead of development. When it does, it impels or awakens a whole series of functions that are in a stage of maturation lying in the zone of proximal development (Vygotsky, 1987, p. 212 as cited in Wilson & Devereux, 2014).

In addition to hints and coaching, performance feedback can be an important component of scaffolding, particularly if it includes "rich dialogic feedback" in which the learner and instructor interact to clarify and discuss aspects of the learning experience and its meaning (Lillis, 2001; Price et al., 2010). By feedback, we mean messages provided to the learner about the correctness of their actions. Feedback can be provided during and after a scenario. Feedback that provides effective scaffolding will engage the learner in productive learning rather than focusing on correcting surface errors. Feedback can vary in terms of its level of specificity, information content, and frequency and timing. These aspects can also be adapted to individual learners. In general, specific feedback is preferable to more general feedback (Earley et al., 1990; Lindsley et al., 1995; Wofford & Goodwin, 1990). The information provided in feedback can be process oriented or outcome oriented. They are closely related to the concepts of "knowledge of results" and "knowledge of performance" used in learning motor skills (Lauber & Keller, 2014). Process-oriented feedback shows learners how to improve their assessments and actions (i.e., "You were unable to complete the rescue mission due to damage to the helicopter from enemy fire requiring an emergency landing. The excessive damage was a result of flying at an altitude that made your helicopter highly visible to potential threats on the ground. In this instance, flying high was riskier than flying low because . . ."). Outcome-oriented feedback focuses on the *results* of the learner's performance (i.e., "You were unable to complete the rescue mission due to damage to the helicopter from enemy fire requiring an emergency landing."). Process-oriented feedback is recommended when new task strategies are being learned (Earley et al., 1990) and may be faded into outcome-based feedback when the learner has demonstrated a degree of proficiency with those strategies. The frequency and timing of feedback can also be varied for different learners, though there is less consensus on how specifically to tailor these to different stages of learning. Mikulincer (1989) suggests that feedback should be less frequent during early stages of skill development. Lindsley et al. (1995) recommend that feedback is best presented contiguous with a performance episode rather than at a later time.

7.1.2   Why Is Scaffolding Important?

The notion of scaffolding acknowledges that much learning is social and involves collaboration between a learner and a more able partner (Luckin & Du Boulay, 1999). It emphasizes the notion that it is important for the instructor to tailor the training difficulty and feedback to the learner's current knowledge and skills. Whether provided by instructor, mentor, or an automated intelligent tutor, well-designed scaffolding can advance learners more effectively than they would on their own. Scaffolding may seem an obvious and natural part of instruction; yet, developing effective scaffolding is not straightforward and many training applications suffer from a lack of appropriate scaffolding.

Without appropriate scaffolding, there is a risk of creating training that is frustrating and demoralizing for beginners and boring for more experienced learners. John Carroll (2014) describes training created at IBM in the early days of microcomputing and word processors that was so challenging it left skilled clerical workers defeated. The experience inspired him to explore new strategies for training that he termed minimalist instruction. Although not framed as scaffolding, minimalist instruction focused on identifying common errors and concerns and developing cards with hints to help learners complete tasks beyond their current "zone of capability" (Wass et al., 2011). With practice, the learners would become less dependent on the cards and the scaffolding could be removed.

Similarly, training that presents experiences and concepts that are low challenge may be considered irrelevant or uninteresting. Learners tend to lose engagement when training is perceived as low-value busy work (Wilson & Devereux, 2014). Most of us can recall a training experience that falls into this category and the associated loss of motivation.

Yet another risk of inappropriate scaffolding is use of support strategies that do not encourage active learning. This can result in dependency on the scaffold itself. Poorly designed support may result in students who learn to accomplish tasks with hints but are not able to accomplish them on their own (Wilson & Devereux, 2014). It is important to withdraw scaffolding as learners demonstrate increasing proficiency to give them opportunities to apply knowledge and skills independently without additional support.

7.1.3 Examples and Empirical Support

Scaffolding is widely used by teachers in educational settings from elementary school to university courses. It has also been integrated into intelligent tutoring systems and other training technologies. There are two core components for effective scaffolding. First, there must be effective scaffolding techniques. These are developed and applied creatively in different training contexts. Human instructors develop strategies for providing hints, directing attention, and developing curricula that scale difficulty level appropriately. Training technologies are sometimes leveraged to provide novel, compelling scaffolding through use of videos, augmented reality, or virtual reality.

Second, there must be effective strategies for assessing the learner's current knowledge, flaws in understanding, and learning needs in order to apply appropriate scaffolding at the right time to create a high-challenge, high-support experience. Skilled instructors are generally able to assess whether the level of challenge is sufficient. They notice when a student is becoming frustrated, bored, or otherwise disengaged. Based on these ongoing assessments of student performance and engagement, skilled instructors determine what type of hint or other scaffolding support might be most helpful. In contrast, incorporating such a broad range of assessments into automated training technologies such intelligent tutoring systems can be challenging though emerging research provides intriguing possibilities for automatically detecting engagement and boredom (Allen et al., 2016; D'Mello et al., 2017; San Pedro et al., 2013). We find examples of intelligent tutoring systems particularly interesting. Because the development of intelligent tutoring systems requires developers to articulate and make visible scaffolding strategies, we find them instructive in exploring scaffolding strategies for both instructor-led and independent learning. (See Woolf [2008] for an in-depth treatment of intelligent tutoring systems and adaptive scaffolding.)

One promising approach to embedding scaffolding in an intelligent tutor is the Intelligent Tutoring Authoring and Delivery System, or ITADS (Ramachandran et al., 2016). This tutor was designed to train troubleshooting skills to US Navy personnel who are learning to provide information technology (IT) support on Navy ships. Intelligent tutoring systems are student-centered, computer-based training systems that are designed to assess the learning needs of each individual learner and provide tailored instruction, much like a human tutor (Woolf, 2008). The ITADS tutor provides problem-based learning opportunities in the form of realistic scenarios to fill the gap between classroom learning and on-the-job performance. For the ITADS software to provide effective scaffolding and feedback, it tracks student actions. Observable actions, however, do not provide enough information. To provide truly targeted feedback, the tutor must have insight into the learner's underlying rationale for their actions. To avoid creating a lengthy and artificial task for learners that would require typing out their rationale for specific actions, ITADS designers introduced a list of hypotheses about the current problem the learner was trying to solve. Learners were asked to select which hypotheses were plausible explanations for the current situation and indicate those that could be ruled out. To maintain high-challenge conditions, as students gained skill they were asked to select appropriate ones from a much larger list of hypotheses. The rationale tracking intervention served both as an assessment and scaffolding mechanism. It provided the trainer a window into a student's troubleshooting knowledge and reasoning process. This enabled the trainer to customize its feedback to the information it gathered. Rationale tracking also served as a scaffolding by prompting students on the potential set of hypotheses they should be tracking and providing ongoing feedback on their reasoning and inferences. The ITADS software uses the learner's hypotheses to identify flaws in the learner's understanding and provide timely and targeted feedback. In a formative evaluation, ten students used the ITADS trainer over ten days. Investigators found that using the tutor resulted in decreased time to solve a problem and that students using the tutor particularly valued the hypothesis-eliciting framework for scaffolding their reasoning process. Figure 7.1 shows the ITAD simulator with a virtual Information Technology (IT) environment on the right and three scaffolding panels on the left. The panel, called the Rationale Panel, in the middle includes a pre-selected list of hypotheses or rationales provided by ITADS. Students are encouraged to use the rationales to perform evidence-gathering actions in the virtual environment and use the results to confirm or refute the hypotheses until they converge on a single one to explain the observed fault in the environment. Figure 7.2 shows an enlarged view of the rationale panel. Note the buttons for confirming/refuting each rationale. Each such action results in feedback about the correctness of the action and an explanation tying the feedback to the evidence gathered by the trainee.

ITADS also includes multi-turn dialogs with the virtual tutor to explore different "what-if" scenarios that are variations of the one just completed. This provides another technique for implementing a form of the Many Variations Principle. Figure 7.3 shows a conceptual example of one such

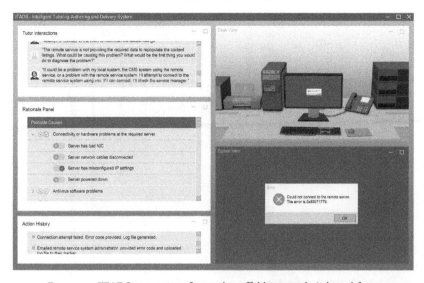

Figure 7.1 ITADS trainer interface with scaffolding panels (adapted from Ramachandran et al., 2016)

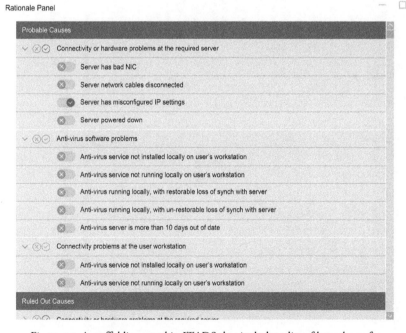

Figure 7.2 A scaffolding panel in ITADS that includes a list of hypotheses for trainees to investigate and either confirm or refute (adapted from Ramachandran et al., 2016)

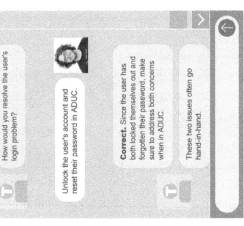

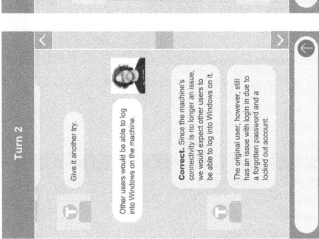

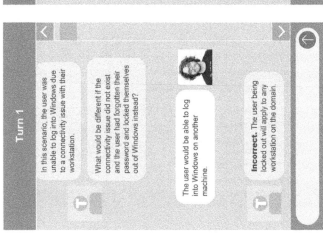

Figure 7.3 Example of a "what if" dialog with the ITADS virtual tutor to discuss a variation of a just-completed scenario (adapted from Ramachandran et al., 2016)

dialog. Note that at each step in the dialog, learners would be presented with a set of response options.

Another intelligent tutor developed for the US Navy is the Tactical Action Officer Intelligent Tutoring System (TAO ITS) (Stottler et al., 2006). TAO ITS was developed as the Navy transitioned from a training model that included one instructor for every two trainees, to a model in which a single instructor would be responsible for forty-two trainees as they independently completed simulated exercises. An important goal was to develop an intelligent tutor that would provide real-time scaffolding. The learner is in the role of the tactical action officer and TAO ITS includes automated team members that operate a Navy ship's weapons, sensors, navigation, and support systems in the Command Information Center. The automated team members provide updates to the tactical action officer to inform his tactical decision-making, and the learner is responsible for monitoring these inputs, maintaining a big-picture view of the situation, and taking appropriate actions as the situation unfolds. Scaffolding is presented via real-time automated coaching in the form of hints designed to help students in the most challenging portions of each scenario. There are four levels of hints, beginning with a flag that appears at the bottom of the screen indicating that some action is expected of the tactical action officer and progressing through increasingly specific hints. During the scenario, when the learner initially misses a cue, the flag pops up indicating an action is required. If the learner fails to act, a more pointed hint appears (e.g., when this type of thing happens, do this). The hints get increasingly specific until the fourth level is reached and the prompt tells the learner exactly what should be done, and the simulation pauses until the appropriate action is taken. Hints and prompts are also provided by simulated teammates and faded as learners demonstrate higher levels of proficiency.

Another interesting example is a tutor called Ecolab, designed to support child learners in collaborating with an intelligent tutoring system to learn about food chains (Luckin & Du Boulay, 1999). To build scaffolding into the Ecolab software they needed to define the range of scaffolding tools to include in the tutor – called the Zone of Available Assistance. This included elements such as manipulating the complexity of the food web presented, from a simple chain of food and feeder to more complex webs with multiple types of organisms. Other scaffolding techniques included using simple concrete labels such as thrush versus more abstract labels such as omnivore or secondary consumer, depending on the learner's current knowledge and skill level. The tutor also included activities intended to call the learner's attention to specific relationships. For example, the learner might be asked to see how many links they can add to a specific food web diagram.

A second key element in Ecolab was to develop strategies for determining the learner's educational needs at any point in time to select which scaffolding elements to present or withdraw – called the Zone of Proximal Adjustment (Luckin & Du Boulay, 1999). As the learner worked through various activities, the Ecolab tutor would provide graded help based on the learner's needs. The highest level of help left the least opportunity for the learner to fail. For example, this might include direct instruction: "Thistle isn't the right sort of organism. Let's try rose-leaves." Conversely, the lowest level of help might point out errors, but not offer a solution: "Caterpillar does not eat thistle. Try again." An evaluation study explored three different approaches to defining what level of challenge and how much support or scaffolding was needed (i.e., Zone of Available Assistance). They found that different strategies worked better for learners at different skill levels. Low skill learners showed greater performance gains when the learner was responsible for selecting the next activity and level of help; average skill learners did best when Ecolab made selections; and high skill learners did best when Ecolab made suggestions about which activity and level of help to choose next. Because it was a small sample study, these findings are difficult to interpret and generalize; however, the authors of the study concluded that providing effective scaffolding that challenges the learner appropriately requires a balance between system (or instructor) direction and learner-driven choices.

Table 7.1 summarizes the ways in which feedback was implemented across these examples to illustrate how type and timing of scaffolding and feedback have been combined in the context of intelligent tutoring systems. These are just a few examples that highlight the many possible strategies and combinations of strategies. Note that certain themes are common across all examples while others vary. Progressing from simple scenarios to complex ones is a common technique found in adaptive training systems. The practice of providing multi-level hints is also common to many ITSs. The examples also illustrate that there are many different, creative ways to provide scaffolding and adaptation, and systems may effectively focus on a small subset of them. ITADS adapts both scaffolding and feedback to learner expertise whereas TAO ITS focuses on adapting along the scaffolding dimension and implementing a more

Table 7.1 *Examples of adaptive scaffolding and feedback techniques implemented in training systems*

Type of Learner	Type and timing of scaffold	Type and timing of feedback
ITADS: Troubleshooting information technology		
Novice	Learners provided with a pre-populated list of potential problems that they can refute/confirm through evidence gathering. Multi-level hints provided upon request.	Feedback when the learner confirms/refutes a hypothesis. Process-oriented feedback at the end of each scenario.
Skilled learner	Learners expected to create their own list of hypothesized problems based on descriptions of initial symptoms. Multi-level hints provided upon request.	Feedback when the learner confirms/refutes a hypothesis. Outcome-oriented feedback at the end of each scenario.
TAO ITS: Navy command and control tactical decision-making		
Novice	Simple scenarios with embedded hints and prompts. Multi-level hints automatically provided when learner is observed to be experiencing difficulties. Prompts from simulated team members.	Process-oriented feedback at the end of each scenario.
Skilled learner	Scenarios with many dimensions of increasing complexity. Multi-level hint automatically provided when learner is observed to be experiencing difficulties.	Process-oriented feedback at the end of each scenario.
Ecolab: Learning conceptual knowledge about food chains		
Novice learner	Simple scenarios with simple food chains. Learners responsible for selecting next activity and level of help.	Outcome-oriented feedback when child "runs" the ecosystem. Outcome-oriented feedback when learner incorrectly defines what a specific animal will eat. Five levels of feedback from direct to abstract.
Mid-level learner	More complex scenarios with multiple types of organisms. System automatically selects next activity and level of help.	Outcome-oriented feedback when child "runs" the ecosystem.

Table 7.1 (cont.)

Type of Learner	Type and timing of scaffold	Type and timing of feedback
		Outcome-oriented feedback when learner incorrectly defines what a specific animal will eat. Five levels of feedback from direct to abstract. Learner sees which animals eats which other animals and plants.
Skilled learner	More complex scenarios with multiple types of organisms. System suggests next activity and level of help.	Outcome-oriented feedback when child "runs" the ecosystem. Outcome-oriented feedback when learner incorrectly defines what a specific animal will eat. Five levels of feedback from direct to abstract. Learner sees which animals eat which other animals and plants.

sophisticated hinting strategy (e.g., providing prompts from simulated teammates). Ecolab provides an interesting method to adapt the amount of control provided to learners in charting their learning path while providing outcome-based feedback for all. The types of scaffolding, feedback and adaptation included in a training system are often determined by the domain or topic of training, availability of resources, and importantly, on what experienced trainers in the field understand to be effective teaching practices.

In addition to these practical examples from the intelligent tutoring community, many researchers have found support for the notion that effective training must be tailored to the learner's proficiency level. For example, Fiore et al. (2008) found that corrective feedback and mentoring is more beneficial at the beginner/apprentice level because it helps less knowledgeable learners overcome incorrect assumptions and a tendency to ignore or explain away information that does not fit in their mental model. However, once learners have advanced beyond the early apprentice level, they need to broaden their experience by applying the principles they have learned in different scenarios and contexts, creating new challenges that allow them to identify and correct limitations and flaws in their mental models. Research indicates that beginners learn better from successful outcomes because they need guidance in figuring out what to do. However, advanced learners learn better from failures because they are better equipped to use the information provided in errors that led to failures (Hoffman et al., 2010).

The design principles articulated in previous chapters support the design of adaptive training. For example, in considering the Periphery Principle, designers can build an adaptive trainer that adds cues that are easily missed and misinterpreted as a student's learning evolves. The Perturbation Principle also suggests a strategy for adaptive training. The trainer can provide beginners with problems involving routine situations and cues and introduce challenging perturbations as the learner's performance advances. The Many Variations Principle similarly supports adaptation to evolving learner expertise as the learner practices assessing and reacting to variable presentations of the type of challenge.

Augmented reality offers interesting possibilities for extending the role of scaffolding in both instructor-led and stand-alone training incorporating intelligent tutors. Avatars in the form of peers or supervisors can be used to encourage learners to articulate rationales, hypotheses, and other components of mental model (see Section 6.1) while still retaining immersion in a training scenario. This information provides insight into the flaws in the learner's understanding and can inform the Zone of Proximal Adjustment. Augmented reality offers a platform for immersive scenarios with different levels and types of challenges. It enables the creation of a range of hints and prompts, including attention-directing comments from an avatar (e.g., "Have you checked the patient's pulse?"), attention-directing visual aids (e.g., pointers to specific cues; comparisons between healthy and injured anatomy), and links between concepts and concrete cues (e.g., animations depicting the asymmetric rise and fall of the chest, jugular vein distention, and tracheal deviation associated with late-stage tension pneumothorax commonly described in texts but rarely seen in the real world). Many augmented reality technologies allow for recording and playback of the learner's view throughout a scenario that can be leveraged in debrief sessions to promote reflection so that learning experiences are more likely to influence future performance. Yet another strategy for leveraging augmented reality to support scaffolding may be in the context of team-based tabletop exercises. Each team member could obtain individualized and private, role- and skill-based support via an augmented reality avatar on a handheld tablet or smartphone platform.

As an example of the value of augmented reality in providing a hint, Figure 7.4 shows the correct placement to insert a needle to relieve pressure from a tension pneumothorax within the chest cavity (a procedure known as needle decompression). Tension pneumothorax is a life-threatening emergency requiring urgent treatment. The procedure consists of finding the mid-clavicular line using the nipple as a guide, then locating the second intercostal space (between the second and third rib). The needle is inserted just lateral to the mid-clavicular line. The guides and message superimposed on the patient amplify a textual description of the process with visuals.

The images in Figure 7.5 show another feature of augmented reality – the ability to "see" under the surface. In the images, a virtual patient's skin is "peeled back" to show underlying anatomy. The first image shows the right lung fully inflated. The second image shows the right lung collapsed, which if left untreated could develop into a tension pneumothorax. Augmented reality could show the progression of the untreated injury as the space around the right lung fills with air, pushing the trachea to one side (tracheal deviation), and the jugular veins distend. Some experienced trainers have found that realistic but idealized illustrations are more effective than photographs for training novices because salient information can be presented, and distracting cues can be de-emphasized. Augmented reality allows for increasingly

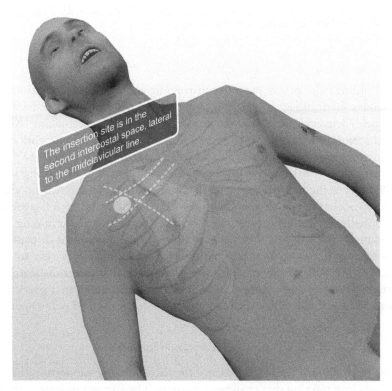

Figure 7.4 Example of a visual guide to explain a procedure

(a)   (b)

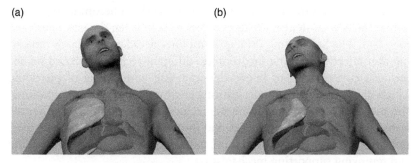

Figure 7.5 Example of using augmented reality to depict features under the surface by virtually "peeling back the skin" to show internal anatomy

realistic presentations of virtual patients and equipment to support scaffolding for different skill levels.

7.1.4   Links to Macrocognition

Scaffolding helps people learn to construct meaning and make decisions in complex environments as described by the recognition-primed decision model (Klein et al., 2010) and the data-frame model of sensemaking (Klein et al., 2006b). Knowing what to attend to and creating meaning are core components of recognition skills and sensemaking. Developing these skills is facilitated by exposure to challenging experiences and also strong scaffolding. For the high-stakes, dynamic domains we are interested in, challenging scenarios can be overwhelming, discouraging, and even dangerous (especially in live-action exercises) without appropriate scaffolding for beginners. Because much of the core skill in these domains is difficult to observe, it is critical that scaffolding techniques include access to the recognition skills of experts. Scaffolding strategies that direct the learner's attention to key cues, clusters of cues, and their meaning in a particular context help build robust mental models needed for skilled performance.

7.1.5   Summary and Discussion

The Scaffolding Principle advocates for incorporating supporting mechanisms into training that challenges learners. The concept of scaffolding is based on Vygotsky's zone of proximal development, in which instructors push learners beyond their current knowledge state. Appropriate scaffolding allows learners to stretch their knowledge without becoming frustrated (when the new content is too difficult) or bored (when the new content is too easy). The Scaffolding Principle amplifies decades of research indicating that effective training incorporates different techniques based on the learner's current level of knowledge and skill with a goal of providing a high-challenge, high-support learning environment. Practically speaking, this means that content and training techniques should vary based on the learner's current proficiency level, and should be designed to push learners to higher proficiency levels and more independence by strategically adding and removing supporting mechanisms.

Human instructors generally develop expertise at assessing the learner's knowledge, skill, confusions, and deficiencies; creating curricula of increasing challenge; and creatively applying a range of learning scaffolds tailored to specific learners and learning environments. Important progress has been made in incorporating these same scaffolding components within intelligent tutoring systems. Researchers continue to explore strategies to develop software that can assess learners' current understanding and apply appropriate scaffolding to correct misconceptions and knowledge gaps. Augmented reality offers a platform to incorporate scaffolding into immersive training scenarios whether they are facilitator-led or stand-alone training via intelligent tutoring systems. Training designers can use augmented reality to create novel scaffolding strategies for prompting, hinting, and debriefing learners.

The Scaffolding Principle can be applied to training all components of recognition skills. Hints to direct attention to critical cues can help learners know what to attend to. Encouraging learners to articulate their rationales can help them make connections among cues and create meaning. Guidance during a simulated scenario or during the simulation debrief can help learners evaluate what they experienced and prepare them for similar situations in the future.

7.1.6 Implications for Training Design

The purpose of scaffolding is to provide an appropriate level of challenge for learners. Interventions such as hints and prompts can also be used as a way to reinforce important concepts and connections. For example, the ITADS example described in Section 7.1.3 includes a scaffold in the form of a rationale panel that also reinforces the links between causes and effects in an IT environment.

Developing adaptive interventions for scaffolding requires more effort than simple one-size-fits-all interventions but does not necessarily require advanced techniques such as artificial intelligence or machine learning to be effective. Techniques such as multi-level hinting that fade as the learner demonstrates increasing proficiency require sophisticated domain knowledge more than complex computational approaches.

Though fine-grained assessments of learner knowledge and proficiency can help deliver highly targeted scaffolding and feedback, even somewhat coarse-grained assessments can lead to effective customizations. For example, asking learners to show or describe the steps they take as they work out a problem can provide the insight needed to associate the steps with learning objectives. Hints and feedback messages can be presented based on the learner's need at a particular point in time – an effective type of adaptive scaffolding. Having sufficient depth of knowledge of the domain, however, is essential and including domain experts in the training development team is highly recommended.

✔ Use scaffolding techniques to provide support to learners and to reinforce important concepts and connections.
✔ Consider relatively simple scaffolding techniques such as multi-level hinting that fades as the learner acquires skill.
✔ Design methods to evaluate current learner understanding to present the appropriate level of scaffolding.
✔ Include domain experts in the training development process.

7.2   Reflection Principle

Reflection Principle. Learners who reflect on the training experience are better able to extract insights from the experience and apply them to future performance.

7.2.1   *What Do We Mean by Reflection?*

Reflection refers to the process of re-examining aspects of performance. First introduced by Dewey (1933) the concept of reflection is widely used in training and education. The term is often used loosely to describe many types of reflective activity, including "questioning, thinking, examining, scrutinizing, mental processing and analysis" (Nguyen et al., 2014, p. 1179). Of the many characterizations of reflection presented in the scientific literature, we prefer the simple definition offered by Hatton and Smith (1995, p. 40): "deliberate thinking about action with a view to its improvement" – with one refinement. Reflection is often broader than a specific action, so we replace that word with experience, leaving us with a more inclusive definition: deliberate thinking about an experience with a view to improving one's own performance.

Reflection can occur before, during, and after an experience (Boud & Walker, 1998; Loughran, 2002; Schön, 1987). However, most training focuses on reflection that follows a training experience during the debrief. We take a similar emphasis, in part because recognition skills in dynamic domains generally require rapid assessment and action. Introducing exercises to encourage reflection during a training scenario runs the risk of adding an element of artificiality that may result in negative task transfer. Therefore, we tend to focus on strategies for encouraging the learner to reflect on the training experience *after* completing the training scenario to identify missed cues, flaws in understanding, and hesitations and errors with a goal of realizing insights that will inform future performance. Reflection should not simply focus on whether the outcome was correct or incorrect, but whether the learner accurately assessed the situation, took appropriate steps, or made errors during the simulation (Earley et al., 1990). Reflection often includes hypothetical thinking as the learner is encouraged to consider how the situation may have played out differently if an alternative action were taken, or situational factors were changed (e.g., more or less time pressure, more or less information available, etc.). Training that encourages reflection immediately following a training simulation may improve one's metacognitive skills, in essence teaching learners how to incorporate reflection before, during, and after actions on the job post training (Ericsson, 2004; Ericsson et al., 2006).

We also advocate for reflection activities that include exposure to other perspectives. Debrief activities that provide targeted feedback from instructors and/or discussion with peers, as well as training tools that facilitate comparison to expert performance are effective strategies for promoting reflection.

7.2.2 Why Is Reflection Important?

The research literature in the domain of expertise explains that one thing that differentiates experts from others is their tendency to reflect on their experiences and seek feedback (Ericsson, 2004; Ericsson et al., 2006). Experts take time to speculate on how situations could have unfolded differently, and extract any lessons learned that can be applied to future situations. Training learners to actively reflect after simulated scenarios can help develop this important metacognitive skill.

For adults, training is often squeezed in between other responsibilities and commitments. It may be necessary to complete a training session and immediately turn attention to other activities. Including activities that facilitate reflection as part of the training session increases the likelihood that learners will take more from the session than simply walking through the steps. Rather, they will have an opportunity to consider how they might have done things differently if they could do it again, how their approach and performance differ from others, and whether they agree with perspectives others take in the context of the same scenario.

7.2.3   Examples and Empirical Support

Debriefs, sometimes called after-action reviews, are commonly used in health care, military, sports, firefighting, and many other settings. The structure and content of these sessions vary widely. In an analysis of the most influential conceptualizations of reflections, researchers discovered five core components of effective debriefs (Nguyen et al., 2014):

1. With regard to content, the debrief should address both *thoughts and actions*.
2. With regard to process, learners should be *attentive, critical, exploratory, and iterative*.
3. Underlying both thoughts and actions, reflection should include *examination of one's own mental model*.
4. The debrief should encourage the learner to be *open to change*.
5. The debrief should encourage the learner to *link items 1–4 to themselves*. Learners should be considering their own thoughts and actions; mental models; attention, criticisms, and explorations; and openness to change.

These elements have been instantiated in many different forms. ShadowBox is a training strategy that has been used in a range of domains and tailored to align with work culture and training needs of individual organizations. ShadowBox encourages reflection using two core components: (1) realistic scenarios that create a challenging situation and (2) an expert model that reveals how experts manage key decisions within each scenario. These components have been combined in different ways to facilitate reflection. For example, ShadowBox created a self-study training program for military personnel using these core components: realistic, challenging scenarios, and expert models (Klein & Borders, 2016). This training focused on transitioning from an authoritarian mindset to a collaborative mindset. Scenarios placed learners in a deployed situation in which they were interacting with local civilians and had to make judgments about how to handle potentially risky interactions, including when to make a show of force and when to de-escalate the situation. Learners worked through the scenarios pausing at decision points to rank their choices from a list of options and record their rationale. The responses of an expert panel were revealed after each decision point and learners were prompted to reflect on and record their insights after considering the expert responses. Even without a facilitator-led debrief, participants showed an improvement in how well they matched the expert responses across the four scenarios. One cohort worked through scenarios using pen and paper and improved 28 percent; another worked through scenarios on a web-based platform and improved by 20 percent. Verkuyl and colleagues (2018) reported similar success with a self-debrief for nursing students after interacting with a virtual gaming simulation of a nursing home visit. They found that self-debrief participants appreciated the time to reflect on the experience and they reported that they were more honest and authentic in their responses to probes than they might have been in a group setting (Verkuyl et al., 2018).

Reflection is also a key component of training for elite athletes. A program developed for elite field hockey players emphasized both individual and team-based reflection and encouraged players to take responsibility for their own learning and reflection (Richards et al., 2009). Based on the theory of empowerment (Arai, 1997), sports researchers described four stages to empowering players through reflection (Kidman et al., 2001). In the first stage, coaches question the players to increase self-awareness. In the second stage, players begin to understand their role in the learning process. In the third stage, the players become the decision-makers; they start to ask questions and demonstrate their increased awareness. In the final stage, players take ownership of their own learning process, asking questions, reflecting without prompting, and contributing to the vision and goals for the team. Richards (2005) created a training program designed to facilitate this sort of empowerment of players so that they would drive their own learning. She developed a reflective worksheet that encouraged players to write down critical events that "players identified as a turning point in the game (whether it was exploited or not)" (Richards et al., 2009, p. 357). They recorded their rationale for selecting the incident, a description of the events leading up to the situation and the actual moment when the incident happened, and the outcome or response. The worksheet provided an outline of the field to draw the location of players, and prompted them to think about what they thought, heard, saw, felt, said, and how they moved. Initially, coaches had discussions with individual players after the players completed worksheets, reviewing the incident and discussing actions required to improve per-formance during similar situations in the future. Coaches also facilitated discussion of the player's role in the context of the larger team, often incorporating videos of the critical event into the discussion. These discus-sions provided coaches with important insights to inform tactical planning as they learned about each player's perceived "best role." As trust relation-ships grew and players became more comfortable with this type of reflection, reflection discussions were introduced into team settings. In a team setting, these discussions had the added benefit of promoting shared mental models across the team. By reflecting on a critical event as a team and reviewing recordings of critical incidents together, players learned how the incident was experienced from different perspectives, reached a common understanding of the event, and achieved consensus on most effective actions to prepare for and respond to similar events in the future. In addition to improved performance, coaches reported that players experienced a reduced sense of isolation and had a greater sense of cohesion.

Intelligent tutoring system designers have developed sophisticated strategies for supporting reflection that reduce the time required by instructors, particularly in military settings where access to skilled instructors and training time are expensive resources. For example, the After Action Intelligent Review System (AAIRS) is designed to support instructors in preparing for and facilitating debrief sessions for large-scale team training exercises of combined arms fire support, a traditionally labor-intensive activity (Jensen et al., 2006). An effective after-action review generally requires the facilitator and learner(s) to recall specific segments of the exercise and examine them together. To support this activity, AAIRS records the training mission as it is executed, synchronizing recorded communications with a recording of the simulator interface. To aid the instructor in preparing for the debrief, AAIRS automatically detects training points, and provides sorting and filtering capabilities so the instructor can quickly locate key points in the exercise and order them as desired for the debrief. AAIRS presents events along a visual timeline so that it is easy to see the sequence of events from different perspectives and identify errors. Voice communications are placed on the timeline, making it clear what was said (and unsaid) before and after key events. For example, the timeline would make it easy to see whether an indirect fire mission was approved before or after the friendly force ground unit initiated a movement. AAIRS saves instructors the need to review a recording of the entire exercise. Rather, it allows the instructor to begin with the system-generated critical incidents, examine them on the timeline, and review the recorded playback of the events. The instructor can instead devote the limited time available to prioritizing events for discussion, adding events, drawing links across events, and planning for a discussion that will facilitate reflection and insight for the trainees.

A game-based environment for practicing negotiation in cross-cultural contexts called the Bi-Lateral Negotiation application (BiLAT) incorporates reflection exercises into an intelligent tutor with no human instructor

(Kim et al., 2009). This trainer focuses on improving cross-cultural negotiation skills for US Army personnel. The reflective tutor feature presents
a scoreboard at the end of the scenario. The scoreboard includes a text-
based summary, performance scores, and a chronological list of all actions
taken during the meeting. The reflective tutor conducts an interactive
review, replaying key parts of the meeting in the playback window, beginning with the action with the most negative impact and ending with the
best action taken by the learner. For each item reviewed, the reflective tutor
selects a tutor tactic. This might include reiterating feedback given by
a simulated coach during the scenario with lengthier explanations,
a multiple-choice question about why an action taken by the learner was
offensive, or asking the learner to choose an alternative action that would
have worked better in that situation. In an evaluation of BiLAT,
researchers found that learners who had no previous experience negotiating
in a non-Western culture performed significantly better on a situational
judgment test (brief, text-based scenarios with multiple-choice questions
that assess a person's judgment; Whetzel & McDaniel, 2009) after one day
of training using BiLAT.

Augmented reality may support reflection exercises in a number of ways.
One tool designed for training combat medics is an Expert Lens to support
debrief activities. After a scenario, the student can use the Expert Lens to
see the expert's performance compared to their own. Additionally, the
system offers the rationale for why the expert's performance was better.
Figure 7.6 shows a patient with two gunshot wounds (right arm and left
leg). The student chose to wrap the arm and apply a tourniquet on the leg.
As seen in Figure 7.6, the tourniquet is located "high and tight" on the leg
as recommended by military doctrine for care under fire, but the bandage
around the arm is incorrect (marked by a check and an x, respectively).
While the arm wound could be bandaged, it is an inappropriate intervention for the phase of care. The care under fire phase of care includes life-
saving treatments that are administered while there is still an active threat.
Bandaging the arm is too time-consuming for such an environment.

Figure 7.7 shows the expert's interventions for the same patient scenario –
a tourniquet on the arm rather than bandages. Figure 7.8 shows the Expert
Lens. The student can turn the Expert Lens on and see the comparison to the
expert model superimposed over their own responses. In Figure 7.8,
the Expert Lens reveals that the expert would have applied a tourniquet to
the arm wound because the first phase of tactical combat casualty care (i.e.,
care under fire) is to address life-threatening bleeding quickly, then rejoin the
fight. It is assumed that during this care under fire phase, the enemy is still

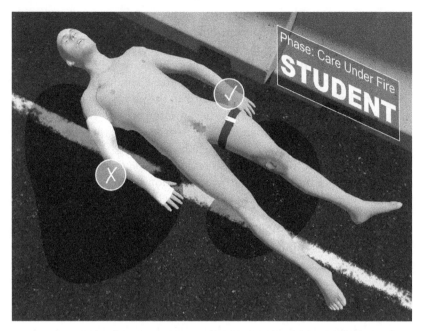

Figure 7.6 Debrief showing one incorrect treatment (bandage around right arm)
and one correct treatment (tourniquet "high and tight" on left leg)

actively engaged, and it is not safe to be heads down carefully
bandaging a wound. Furthermore, if the patient is hemorrhaging,
a tourniquet should be applied quickly; a pressure dressing is unlikely
to be effective.

Many augmented reality platforms create a video recording of the
training scenario from the learner's perspective. The video provides the
instructor (or the intelligent tutor) insight into the learner's attention,
including where the learner was looking at key points in the scenario and
which actions were taken. This recording can also be used to review errors
and missed cues, as well as poorly implemented interventions. These data
can be used to structure a debrief session. They can be used to compare the
learner's strategies and performance to their peers or to an expert model to
see how others may have handled the same situation. These data can be
used to identify teaching points for an independent learner or intelligent
tutor. Augmented reality also makes it possible to replay training scenarios
to explore other paths and outcomes, thereby providing enhanced
opportunities for reflection.

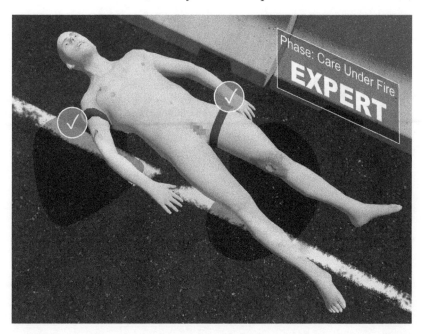

Figure 7.7 Debrief showing the expert's actions for the same patient scenario with correct treatments

7.2.4   *Links to Macrocognition*

The practice of reflection is believed to be a discriminator between experts and nonexperts, as it supports deliberate practice and increases the learning value of each experience (Ericsson et al., 1993). This is particularly important in dynamic, high-stakes domains where decisions are often made under time pressure and in the face of uncertainty. Reflection exercises are designed to help learners make the most of each training experience and take ownership of their own reflection so it becomes a natural part of their training and on-the-job performance (Fadde & Klein, 2010). Reflection may promote metacognitive skills and mental simulation as learners become accustomed to considering other potential paths and outcomes in a given situation, a key component of the recognition-primed decision model. Debrief strategies to support reflection are commonly used in many contexts to refine the skills needed for effective recognition primed decision-making. Debriefs provide the time and structure to consider critical cues that were noticed late or not at

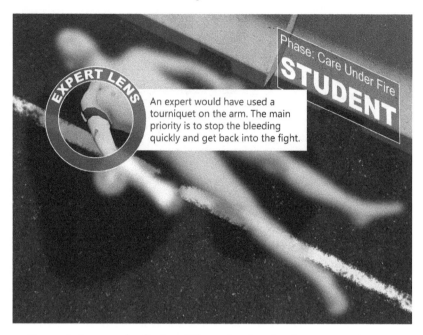

Figure 7.8 Augmented reality-based "Expert Lens" used to show expert actions over
the student's own performance

all, misinterpretations and inaccurate assessments, misaligned goals and
expectancies, and ineffective actions.

7.2.5   Summary and Discussion

The Reflection Principle advocates for developing training experiences that
encourage learners to actively reflect on what they have experienced, how
the situation may have unfolded differently, and how to apply what they
have learned to future situations. We define reflection as *deliberate thinking
about an experience with a view to improving one's own performance.*
Reflection exercises are often incorporated into debrief sessions led by an
instructor or guided by an intelligent tutoring system, although they can
occur before or during a training experience. The goals of reflection are to
evaluate a learner's performance in terms of situation assessment, cue
recognition, judgments, and actions. Reflection can also be used to encourage hypothetical thinking about how changing specific aspects of the
scenario may have altered the situation, and how the learner would have

adapted. Reflection exercises can be used to share other perspectives to help broaden the learner's insights from the training exercise. Training that includes active reflection provides practice that may positively transfer to reflecting on experiences outside of training. The tendency to reflect on one's own performance, whether on the job or in training is one of the hallmarks of expertise.

Debrief activities that incorporate reflection support the development of recognition skills in terms of revisiting cues that may have been missed and discussing whether the learner drew appropriate conclusions about the meaning of the available cues. Reflection can also help learners mentally simulate potential outcomes of actions in future situations, particularly if it includes hypothetical changes to the scenario and alternative perspectives on the same scenario.

Because many augmented reality platforms record the scenario from the learner's point of view, they can aid the facilitator or intelligent tutoring system in understanding what the learner attended to throughout the scenario. This information can be used to compare an individual learner's performance to that of peers or to an expert model. Augmented reality also supports the ability to replay portions of the scenario repeatedly to explore alternate paths. When training in less time-pressured domains, augmented reality can introduce opportunities for reflection during the simulation itself. However, this may interfere with the realism and the learner's engagement with the simulation.

7.2.6 *Implications for Training Design*

Reflection exercises can be incorporated at different points in a training program. For training recognition skills where learner engagement and immersion is important, reflection is generally emphasized at the end of scenarios as a part of after-action review. Including reflection at the conclusion of scenarios enables the use of in-depth exploration activities such as discussing rationales, the impact of action choices on the outcomes, and alternate courses of actions.

There may also be opportunities to embed activities related to reflection into the training scenario. The ShadowBox trainer described in Section 7.2.3 is an example where the objective was to train decision-making skills in a context where immersion was de-emphasized in favor of deliberation. Here the mental model prompts encourage reflection at key decision points in the scenario. Learners are asked to think through the priorities and risks impacting their decisions in the moment. Where reflection activities are placed and how many are used depends on the training objectives and the desired learning outcomes.

The strategies for prompting reflection can also be varied. One approach is to replay scenarios, stopping at critical moments to elicit reflection. The BiLAT example in Section 7.2.3 suggests organizing reflection activities based on a rank order of learner actions from those that most negatively influenced outcomes to those that most positively influenced outcomes. In the context of team training, reflection might include reviewing the scenario from the perspective of different roles as described by Richards' (2005) work with elite field hockey players.

Another important consideration is whether tailored feedback is to be provided for reflection activities. This question is particularly critical for stand-alone training approaches such as intelligent tutoring systems. Some have advocated for developing algorithms that can automatically process learner input at a deep enough level of understanding to generate tailored feedback. One purpose of reflection is to provide an opportunity for free-ranging analysis of one's actions. This type of input is difficult for an automated system to comprehend at a deeper level. However, in many cases a simpler approach may be effective. Providing an opportunity to reflect and compare one's responses with expert responses and rationale (i.e., an expert model) is one approach that has been effective.

✔ Incorporate reflection exercises at the end of a training scenario to maintain immersion, or throughout the training if immersion is less important based on training goals.

✔ Include strategies to prompt learners to reflect, for example, replaying a scenario, evaluating actions in terms of impact, and reviewing actions from a different perspective.

✔ Explore strategies for prioritizing which aspects of performance to highlight in after-action-review and debrief exercises.

✔ Consider incorporating an expert model so that learners can compare their own actions to an expert's.

CHAPTER 8

Synthesis

The eleven design principles described in this book can be instantiated in training in many ways, limited only by imagination and resources. In this chapter, we share our experiences implementing these principles in the context of augmented reality training. It is important to note that the label "augmented reality training" may be misleading in that it implies training that is completely built using augmented reality technology. It is easy for training developers to focus exclusively on the augmented reality experience and neglect to leverage other available learning media to create an integrated learning experience. (In fact, some of our early training designs fell into this trap.)

To avoid this problem going forward, we have adopted the Learn, Experience, Reflect framework to guide our training design. Augmented reality training experiences, or really any scenario-based training experience, cannot exist in a vacuum. Each experience must be supported by didactic components that lay the foundation for the training. We call this the Learn component. This might include explaining concepts, providing definitions, describing procedures, and presenting instructions for using the training technology. The Learn component can motivate learners by showing the connection between the training and real life. It can also set up performance expectations. The Experience component focuses on presenting the learner with challenging scenarios; many of the design principles in this handbook are aimed at creating compelling and instructional Experience components. Experiences must also be integrated into the learner's existing knowledge structures. The Reflect component focuses on drawing connections between existing and new knowledge and skills.

The Learn, Experience, Reflect framework encourages the multidisciplinary design team to articulate:

- What declarative information the learner will need to make the most of the training experience;

- What experiences to provide that will support the learner in applying abstract concepts to real-world challenges; and
- What strategies to use to help the learner reflect on what they have learned and consider how it might influence their actions going forward.

Our training design teams often include human factors psychologists who conduct cognitive task analyses to understand the cues and strategies experienced practitioners use to quickly size up a situation and act under time pressure, the complexities and perturbations they manage, and the common errors that occur. The human factors psychologists work with software developers, training designers, and skilled practitioners in the domain of interest (e.g., combat medics, emergency department physicians, military aviators, etc.) to determine how to use the findings from the cognitive task analysis to develop effective augmented reality-based training using the design principles described in this handbook. The Learn, Experience, Reflect framework has become a valuable resource for supporting collaboration and communication across the multidisciplinary training development team.

It is important to point out that Learn, Experience, and Reflect are not discrete components that are necessarily presented in a linear format. Learn components can be combined with Experience components in the form of hints and tutorials. Reflect components are often combined with Experience components when learners are provided direct feedback and given an opportunity to repeat the experience or replay a portion of the scenario. The framework is a mechanism to ensure that Learn, Experience, and Reflect activities are included in the training experience; the intent is not to constrain the training activities used or to suggest that Learn components must come first and Reflect activities must come last. Next, we discuss each component of the framework in turn.

8.1   Learn, Experience, Reflect Framework

8.1.1   Learn

The *Learn* component refers to strategies for presenting declarative information such as facts and concepts. These can often be effectively conveyed in text, lecture, or video presentation. This might include an explanation of how the training platform works and what is expected of the learner, learning objectives to prepare the learner for the training activities, and procedures and key concepts relevant to the learning objectives. These elements become particularly important in the context of stand-alone training, where there is no instructor present to elaborate and respond to questions or create enthusiasm for the topic using stories and an engaging, interactive presentation style.

The Learn component can support engagement by explaining to the learner the value of the skills to be trained. For example, a training program focused on recognizing and correcting ineffective tourniquets might begin by sharing statistics about the number of people who die due to ineffective tourniquet placement, and how many lives are saved as a result of correct tourniquet placement. Highlighting that this training may improve the learner's ability to save lives can increase engagement and support immersion as described by the Scenario Immersion Principle in the chapter on Engagement.

In the TALSAR application described in Sections 3.1 and 5.1 on the Scenario Immersion and Sensory Fidelity Principles, the Learn component presents text-based learning objectives designed to engage combat medic learners by linking the learning objectives to operational challenges. For example, when deployed to a region with venomous animals, the learner might find learning objectives related to recognizing and treating envenomation. When given an assignment that involves treating civilians such as a humanitarian relief mission, the learner might choose learning objectives related to recognizing and treating traumatic brain injury in children. In addition to preparing the learner for an immersive experience by making it clear that the training topics are relevant to challenges the learner will likely face, the Learn component of TALSAR also sets the stage for supporting mental models by presenting clear, concise job aids that include key facts and concepts presented in the form of easy-to-remember mnemonics. These key facts and concepts build on the learners' existing mental models, highlighting how pediatric head injuries differ from the adult head injuries that combat medics assess and treat routinely. Furthermore, these job aids are paired with annotated visual references that highlight critical cues the learner will practice recognizing in the experiential learning phase.

In short, regardless of training media, Learn components of training can prepare the learner for engaging in the training, and build on existing mental models to support an immersive training experience that facilitates mental model development and elaboration.

8.1.2 Experience

Augmented reality offers broad scope for creating experiential learning elements. Many of the principles described in this handbook support the Experience component of the framework. The Scenario Immersion

Principle advocates for compelling, realistic scenarios, and the Hot Seat Principle suggests strategies for putting the learner in the role of decision-maker. The Periphery and Perturbation Principles provide guidance for scenario design. The Sensory and Scaling Fidelity Principles highlight the importance of presenting realistic cues at scale to support perceptual skill development. The Mental Model Articulation and Many Variations Principles describe strategies for supporting mental model construction. The Scaffolding Principle describes strategies to support learners in participating in experiences that stretch beyond their current skills.

These principles can be woven into training in many different combinations. Very short scenarios that represent a snapshot in time can be used to present many variations, highlighting important sensory cues at scale. This type of flashcard approach can be used to juxtapose similar cues to aid learners in differentiating cues that are commonly confused. Flashcards can be used to show many variations of virtual patients with a specific injury (e.g., gunshot wounds) or environmental cues needed to recognize weather conditions in-flight (see description of Weatherwise by Wiggins & O'Hare [2003] in Chapter 5).

Other types of learning objectives are better served by scenarios that unfold over time. If the intent is for learners to understand how a patient's condition might evolve or how a weather system can develop, a flashcard approach will not be sufficient. Scenarios that extend over time are more conducive to the Scenario Immersion Principle as learners have more support for imagining themselves in the situation presented. This effect can be amplified by placing learners in the hot seat where they are responsible for problem-solving and decision-making. Augmented reality provides a platform for presenting high-fidelity sensory cues at scale in the context of a scenario that unfolds over time.

Determining which cues and what types of perturbations to include in the training scenarios is largely guided by the challenges practitioners will face on the job, and an understanding of cues and strategies used by experienced practitioners – often informed by cognitive task analysis. These will be reflected in the learning objectives articulated in the Learn component and instantiated in the Experience component. For example, the US military has identified three common battlefield injuries that are potentially deadly and also highly treatable: airway obstruction, tension pneumothorax, and hemorrhage. These have become overarching learning objectives for training for different levels of combat medicine (Butler, 2017). Cognitive task analysis can be used to explore important questions to guide training design. These include questions such as: What makes these types of injuries and their severity difficult to recognize and treat? What cues do experienced medics use to assess patients, especially in challenging situations? What strategies are used to treat patients in a range of conditions from care under fire to tactical field care to tactical evacuation to care in a hospital setting? Unpacking the real-world complexities and expert cues and strategies is critical to effective recognition skills training in high-stakes domains. Learning a standard procedure is not enough; training must prepare learners to assess and act in the context of the complexities and perturbations they will face in the real world. This in-depth, context-rich domain knowledge can inform detailed, specific learning objectives and aid in designing scenarios that include realistic perturbations such as missing or broken equipment, unexpected weather conditions, and inexperienced team members.

The Experience component also provides an important platform for scaffolding and feedback. Hints can be used to support learners in working through scenarios that are beyond their current skill level. Prompts can be used to encourage learners to articulate aspects of their mental models such as assessments, goals, and planned actions. Immediate feedback can help learners see the flaws in their thinking. Augmented reality makes it easy to replay a scenario if learners decide to try a different path after seeing the results of their actions. To retain a sense of immersion, hints, and prompts can come from a virtual colleague or supervisor who directs the learner's attention or asks for a status update.

8.1.3 Reflect

The Reflect component refers to explicit reflection activities that support integration of new knowledge and skills. Although scaffolding and feedback during the Experience component are likely to support reflection, we also advocate for deliberate Reflect exercises that take place immediately following the Experience component. Different domains refer to this as a debrief, after-action review, or hotwash, all of which incorporate important aspects of the Reflection Principle. These Reflect sessions are often led by instructors and may include individual learners or an entire team. The challenge for the instructor is to identify learning points and facilitate discussion with limited preparation. Domain-specific tools such as AAIRS (described in Chapter 7) are designed to support instructors in preparing for and facilitating after-action reviews. Augmented reality technology may support this process in important ways as the learner's-eye view is easy to record and replay for review. Furthermore, it is possible for an instructor to control what the learner sees using a device such as a tablet. This device can also be used to mark learning points as they occur during the scenario so they can be quickly retrieved to support discussion and reflection.

We also advocate for the use of quizzes and test scenarios as a means for learners to test their own knowledge and identify knowledge gaps – especially in the context of stand-alone training when an instructor is not present. This may include simple multiple-choice knowledge tests based on the key facts and concepts presented during the Learn component. This may also include test scenarios either in the form of flashcards or scenarios that unfold over time. The primary difference from training scenarios is that, in the test scenarios, the learner knows they are testing their own knowledge and skills, and no hinting features are available. The intent is to shift the learner's mindset from a learning mode that might include exploration of how different actions (including errors) might play out and an opportunity to practice and "re-do" specific actions until they are mastered – to a focus on displaying their best performance. After completing knowledge tests and test scenarios, learner responses can be presented in comparison to an expert's approach to the same scenario, along with the expert's rationale. In this way, learners can have access to an expert perspective, even during independent, standalone training.

8.2   Theoretical Links

Throughout this handbook, we provide links to macrocognition as a means to stay grounded in our focus on recognition skills training. Macrocognition is the study of decision-making and other cognitive activities in complex settings. In discussion of each principle, we provide links to the training and cognitive psychology literatures from which the principles were derived. In this synthesis chapter, we consider links to instructional systems design. In particular, Kolb's experiential learning style theory describes a four-stage learning cycle that includes: concrete experience, reflective observation, abstract conceptualization, and active experimentation (Kolb, 1975; McLeod, 2017). We find that the Learn, Experience, Reflect framework aids training designers in creating training that incorporates these four elements in an integrated way. Some approaches focus on a more decompositional approach, defining learning objectives according to Bloom's taxonomy, which suggests that one begins with a straightforward knowledge level of learning and then progresses in complexity through comprehension, application, analysis, synthesis, and evaluation. Each learning objective is categorized in terms of this taxonomy, which informs the training design. Knowledge, comprehension, and analysis are often taught in classroom settings, and analysis, synthesis, and evaluation are often taught on the job (Air Force Manual, 2003). This stratification may be less appropriate for the types of recognition skills we are most interested in; our goal is generally to combine these different levels into an integrated training experience.

Kolb also highlighted four distinct learning styles and points out everyone needs the stimulus of all types of learning styles to some extent. The styles are based on Kolb's experiential learning style theory. The first learning style is diverging, which refers to a learning mode in which the learner observes, gathers information, and uses imagination to solve problems. The second learning style is assimilating, which refers to a learning mode that is concise and logical and is supported by lectures, analytic models, and time to think things through. The third learning style is converging, which refers to a learning mode focused on making practical use of ideas and theories, applying facts and concepts to practical problems. The fourth learning style is accommodating, which refers to a learning mode that relies more on intuition and gut instinct. We find that the Learn, Experience, Reflect framework aids the design team in creating an integrated learning experience that engages each learning style at some point in the experience. Specifically, the Learn component allows for the observation and information gathering described as diverging and the concise logical information presentation supports assimilating. The Experience component engages the converging style by asking the learner to apply facts and concepts in the context of a realistic scenario; scenarios can also be designed to encourage the use of intuitive decision strategies such as recognition-primed decision-making. The Reflect component will likely engage all four learning styles as learners take part in reflective exercises such as working through knowledge tests and test scenarios, and comparing their performance to an expert model.

8.3   Summary and Discussion

The eleven design principles described in this book focus primarily on strategies for creating scenario-based augmented reality training for recognition skills. However, it is important to consider the training elements needed to support the augmented reality experiences to create an integrated learning experience. We have articulated the Learn, Experience, Reflect framework to guide our training design and support collaboration across the multidisciplinary design team.

The Learn component includes the knowledge, facts, and procedures that set the groundwork for effective experiential training. The Experience component is generally scenario-based and can take on many forms. This may include very short flashcard-type scenarios that represent a snapshot in time or scenarios that develop over time. The Reflect component focuses on strategies for supporting the learner in integrating new and existing knowledge and skills.

These components are not necessarily discrete and do not need to be presented in a linear order. They can be combined in creative ways to meet a broad range of learning objectives and accommodate a variety of learning contexts. We find that this framework is compatible with Kolb's (1975) four-stage learning cycle and aids designers in considering activities that incorporate concrete experiences, reflective observation, abstract conceptualization, and active experimentation in an integrated way.

8.4   Implications for Training Design

To avoid getting caught in the trap of focusing on the augmented reality experience exclusively, we recommend the Learn, Experience, Reflect framework as a mechanism for thinking about the training experience more holistically.

To determine what Learn components are necessary, consider what the learner will need to know to get the most out of the Experience component of training and what they are expected to be able to do after training (i.e., the learning objectives). Are there specific facts, concepts, or procedures they must be familiar with before they work through training scenarios? What do they need to know about the training technology and what is expected of them in the training experience to be able to complete the training scenarios? Is there contextual information that will help the learner appreciate the importance of this training and increase engagement?

To create effective Experience components, consider learning objectives and the training context. Important elements of training context include: Where will training take place? Will there be an instructor present? Will it be individual or team training? How much time will learners have available? These contextual elements will constrain design activities, but also provide opportunities for combining the design principles described in this book in creative ways.

The Reflect components are also largely driven by learning objectives and training context. Reflect components can be integrated with Learn and

Experience components and are also commonly included in post-scenario activities to allow for more in-depth exploration and discussion.

✔ It is important to consider the entire training experience when designing recognition skills training, not just the technology.

✔ Use learning objectives and training goals to guide the content for Learn, Experience, and Reflect components of the training.

✔ Consider the context in which the training application will be used. This will guide you in deciding which principles in this book to emphasize and combine.

CHAPTER 9

Conclusion

Augmented reality technologies open the door to a broad range of training approaches. Using handheld and head-worn devices, it is possible to project virtual objects onto nearly any environment, combining elements of the real world with virtual objects to create experiential, scenario-based training anywhere. The resulting experience is generally immersive and engaging, two important components of recognition skills training. We are interested in building on this foundation. The training and education literatures provide important guidance for designing training. The naturalistic decision making and macrocognition literatures provide a theoretical backdrop for understanding recognition skills and insight into skill acquisition. Leveraging these literatures and our own experience developing augmented reality-based training for combat medics, we identified eleven principles to guide training designers. Of course, these are the early days of augmented reality training. As augmented reality technologies continue to become more affordable and overcome some of the current limitations (e.g., limited field of view, limited processing power), we expect to see more augmented reality-based training programs and research endeavors that will extend and refine these principles. Until then, we hope that these principles aid training designers in creating learning experiences to support people working in critical, high-stakes domains who must rapidly assess a situation and take action.

9.1 Eleven Principles for Designing Augmented Reality-Based Recognition Skills Training

The eleven principles for designing augmented reality-based recognition skills training address five important dimensions: engagement, scenario building, fidelity and realism, mental model construction, and scaffolding and reflection. These dimensions form the foundation of recognition skills training. We highlight three components of recognition skills. First,

128

recognition requires knowing what to attend to, including which cues are relevant in which contexts. Second, to recognize a situation and know how to act, learners must be able to create meaning from the cues available. Third, having sophisticated mental models allows learners to evaluate potential interventions before acting by mentally playing them out, also known as mental simulation. The eleven design principles included in this handbook are intended to help learners learn to identify relevant cues and clusters of cues, interpret the situation correctly, and anticipate problems using mental simulation.

The engagement principles focus on strategies for leveraging augmented reality to create a compelling learning experience. The realism of augmented reality sets the stage for an engaging learning experience. The Scenario Immersion Principle advocates for using training scenarios that place the learner in the experience to create a sense of presence or immersion. The Hot Seat Principle goes a step further, recommending strategies for putting the learner in the role of decision-maker to encourage the learner to actively assess the situation and decide what to do in response to challenges presented in the training scenario.

ENGAGEMENT PRINCIPLES

Scenario Immersion Principle: Scenario-based training that creates a sense of the learner's presence in the scenario supports engagement.

Hot Seat Principle: Creating a learning situation in which the learner feels responsible for managing the situation supports recognition skill development.

The scenario-building principles highlight important components of scenario design. We emphasize the importance of training that includes not just the most common and easy-to-detect cues, but also the subtle or peripheral cues. Knowing where to find critical cues, and how to distinguish critical cues from potential distractors is an important component of recognition skills. We also advocate for including scenarios that represent nonroutine conditions. For the types of dynamic, high-stakes environments we are most interested in, learning to adapt and innovate when the unexpected happens is critical to skilled performance. Scenarios in which equipment breaks down, supplies run low, key team members are unavailable or incapacitated, or any number of other perturbations occur, provide a safe space for learners to make mistakes and take risks so that they are equipped to adapt effectively on the job. Augmented reality technologies make it possible to create compelling scenarios. For combat medic training, the patient's condition and other contextual elements can change over time; instructors can choose to make peripheral cues more noticeable over time if they are missed by the learner. Many of the peripheral cues that are difficult to represent with physical manikins or even live actors are easily incorporated into augmented reality. A patient's skin tone and facial expression can change over time as distal perfusion is reduced and the patient begins to lose consciousness. Dynamic cues such as the rise and fall of the chest or bleeding can evolve over the course of the simulation. Because the scenarios are software-based, content is reusable. It is possible to create a basic scenario and add perturbations at relatively low cost and effort.

SCENARIO-BUILDING PRINCIPLES

Periphery Principle: Effective scenarios should include critical cues that are not obvious; rather, the learner must know to look for them and correctly interpret them.

Perturbation Principle: Training scenarios should expose trainees to novel conditions requiring adaptation and performance under non-routine conditions.

The fidelity and realism principles emphasize the value of including realistic sensory cues to support learners in making important perceptual discrimination. When embedded in scenarios, cues can be combined in different ways to provide practice at creating meaning in different contexts. By presenting virtual props at a physical scale close to that of the real world, learners can refine their perceptual skills as they move within the environment and observe from different perspectives. For combat medic training, learners can explore the benefits and drawbacks of different body positioning to best assess the patient and administer interventions. By creating training that incorporates both assessing and acting in the same learning experience, learners can practice attention management. They can more fully experience the need to act even when the assessment is incomplete but time pressure requires action, and the value of reassessing after an action is taken. Augmented reality platforms make it possible to project photorealistic images in nearly any environment to support sensory and scaling fidelity. Although visual fidelity is the most common application of augmented reality, audio and even olfactory cues can be incorporated to engage more senses. By combining virtual and physical assets, innovative strategies for combining assessment and action into the same learning experience become possible.

FIDELITY AND REALISM PRINCIPLES

Sensory Fidelity Principle: Realistic cue presentation is needed to support perceptual skill development.

Scaling Fidelity Principle: Virtual props should be at a scale close to the real world.

Assessment–Action Pairing Principle: It is important to create a learning experience that allows the learner to both assess the situation and act.

The principles to support constructing mental models address one of the fundamental components of recognition skills. To know what cues to look for, to make sense of the information presented, and to mentally simulate potential actions and outcomes, one must have robust mental models. Developing robust mental models generally takes years. Therefore, we focus on strategies to train people to make the most of every experience, to actively construct their own mental models, and to refine and expand their mental models with each new experience. The Mental Model Articulation Principle advocates for using techniques that encourage the learner to say aloud (or write down) components of their mental models. The benefits of this are three-fold. First, to articulate components of a mental model, the learner must actively construct one. Second, by articulating their mental model, flaws become visible to instructors (and to the learner) so they can be examined and corrected. Third, training strategies that encourage learners to articulate aspects of their mental model set the stage for reflection, an important practice for developing and refining recognition skills (see Section 7.2). The Many Variations Principle emphasizes the importance of training that includes many experiences so that learners can begin to see the limits of existing mental models and expand and enrich their mental models appropriately. Often it is possible to take a single training scenario and vary key elements so learners can begin to see how different variables can create a shift in assessment, alter the meaning of other cues, and influence outcomes.

SUPPORTING MENTAL MODEL CONSTRUCTION PRINCIPLES

Mental Model Articulation Principle: Training techniques that require the learner to articulate what they are noticing, how they are assessing the situation, and predictions about how the situation will evolve aid the learner in developing coherent mental models.

Many Variations Principle: Training techniques that expose the learner to many variations with different levels of difficulty support development of robust mental models.

Scaffolding and reflection principles focus on how to support learners during the training experience. The concept of scaffolding recognizes that placing learners in a high–challenge, high-support situation can accelerate learning. The support or scaffolding allows learners to work through problems beyond their current skill level to enable a sort of experiential learning that is difficult to achieve without help. Augmented reality makes it possible to provide scaffolding in flexible and immersive ways. For example, an avatar can play the role of a colleague or mentor that provides attention-directing hints ("Did you check his airway?"). Visual pointers can be superimposed on a virtual or physical asset to highlight specific anatomy or other critical cues. Animations can be presented to show relationships that are difficult to see in the real world (e.g., how external cues are driven by changes in underlying physiology). Furthermore, augmented reality platforms make it possible for an instructor to insert scaffolding components in real time when they see a learner moving in a wrong direction or struggling to solve a problem. Reflection focuses on supporting the learner in extracting insights from each experience. During training, reflection generally occurs when the scenario is complete in the form of a debrief session to avoid disrupting scenario immersion; however, the goal is to encourage the learner to integrate reflection into work in a pervasive way. Many augmented reality platforms create a recording of the learner's-eye view of the scenario as it unfolded; some create gaze tracking data as well. This record of the training event is a powerful tool for revisiting key aspects of the scenario, and for comparing an individual's performance with that of an expert. It is also possible to juxtapose key segments of the scenario to highlight evolving cues. For combat medic training, this type of debrief might include a brief clip of the patient at three different points in the scenario to allow the learner to focus on how skin tone, breathing, and other cues shifted over the course of the scenario.

SCAFFOLDING AND REFLECTION PRINCIPLES

Scaffolding Principle: Student-centered learning support can be used to promote recognition skill development at different skill levels.

Reflection Principle: Learners who reflect on the training experience are better able to extract insights from the experience and apply them to future performance.

9.2 Boundary Conditions for These Design Principles

We have selected design principles that are particularly relevant for training recognition skills in dynamic, high-stakes environments. Our emphasis is on using augmented reality to create immersive, scenario-based training experiences. Although many of these principles were initially created based on research to design education and training for conceptual skills such as math, physics, and chess (Chase & Simon, 1973a; Chi et al., 1994; Devereux & Wilson, 2008; Seel & Dinter, 1995; Vygotsky, 1978), we have adapted them and emphasized aspects that are most relevant for recognition skills training. For more conceptual skills that allow for deliberation and analysis such as math, physics, and chess, scenario immersion may be less important, and therefore the use of avatars to provide hints or ask questions, emphasizing reflection during a debrief rather than in real time and the learner's-eye view recording of the learning experience may be less relevant. Our test bed has been combat medic training where visual cues and dynamic situations are critical to recognition skill development. Trainers focused on tasks for which perceptual skills and an evolving situation are less relevant may find the sensory and fidelity principles to have limited relevance. However, because these principles are derived from training and education across a broad range of domains, we hope that the empirical examples provided offer a solid foundation for training designers as they undertake the creative aspects of design and create new innovations in simulation-based training.

9.3 Augmented Reality Contributions and Challenges

Augmented reality has captured the imagination of the marketing, gaming, and training communities. The ability to augment the physical world with virtual assets introduces a whole range of opportunities to motivate, entertain, and educate. Head-worn platforms allow hands-free operation, and modern smartphones and tablets make augmented reality easy and inexpensive to disseminate. For training designers, the possibilities seem endless. Realistic virtual assets can be integrated into reusable training scenarios. This includes the use of avatars and animations to provide hints and ask questions in order to enhance the learning experience and still remain immersed in the scenario. In addition to creating a compelling, immersive experience, most platforms create a record of the learner's-eye view and many incorporate gaze tracking data, making it possible to track the learner's performance and replay aspects for reflection. The portability of augmented reality platforms means learners are no longer tied to a simulation facility; training can happen anywhere. On the other hand, augmented reality can be integrated into existing simulation facilities to augment and extend physical manikins and other simulation technologies. All sorts of possibilities exist; manikins and augmented reality training can be used in clinical settings, mock battlefields, and other work settings to create "in situ" training. Augmented reality also has the advantage of usability; users do not experience "cyber sickness" found with some virtual reality technologies when what you see misaligns with what your vestibular system tells you is happening (Vovk et al., 2018). With most augmented reality applications, you physically move through space (rather than experience the illusion of movement virtually), so no sickness ensues.

It is important to temper this enthusiasm with pragmatic considerations. Challenges to incorporating augmented reality into training still exist. Initially, it may be difficult to convince a training organization to consider augmented reality-based training, especially in domains where related technology was not native during the formative years. This includes nearly every domain with a training tradition that is more than ten years old. Integrating augmented reality-based training into existing curricula may seem daunting at an organizational level. For those interested in incorporating augmented reality–based training, access to the hardware can be a barrier. Although head-worn devices are increasingly available, they remain expensive and in limited production. Even with an adequate budget, it can be difficult to obtain head-worn devices. Rapidly evolving augmented reality devices have platform-specific limitations. Current head-worn devices have a limited field of view; thus requiring head movements and body positioning that may deviate from real-world operations in some cases. Some of the head-worn platforms are bulky and uncomfortable. In some situations on some devices, the virtual objects occlude important physical objects; learners may not be able to see their own hands if they are hidden behind a virtual object. Glare from bright lights can affect the appearance of virtual objects. Smartphones and tablets are both widely available and relatively inexpensive, but generally require the learner to hold the device, making it difficult to perform physical actions and reducing the sense of immersion. These are important trade-offs to consider when determining which platform to use for training.

From a development perspective, it is also worth noting that some other technologies such as virtual reality tend to have more boundaries which simplifies programming architectures. With augmented reality, it is harder to constrain scenarios to make programming easier because software developers are forced to work with the real world. This leads to challenges in mapping virtual constructs onto real-world objects. Physics, scale, and perspectives matter a lot more. For example, in an augmented reality world where real-world aircraft operate with virtual ships, it is important to get the motion of the ships to be compatible with the real-world motion of the aircraft. Additionally, the virtual and the real are superimposed in a scene, comparisons between the two are easier and the deviations of the virtual from the real become more apparent and possibly more jarring. The benefit, however, is that augmented reality is more flexible, providing a canvas for training developers to experiment with creative and novel training interventions.

With regard to assessing the impact of augmented reality training on on-the-job performance, all of the barriers to meaningful evaluation that are present with other training modalities are still present, and some may be exacerbated. Recognition skills, in particular, are difficult to measure. This is in part because we advocate for training scenarios, scaffolding techniques, and reflection and feedback that are tailored to the skills of the learner. This type of adaptive training means that the training itself varies, making it difficult to determine which components have a positive impact and under which circumstances. Furthermore, improvements in recognition skills are hard to measure. Studies must be designed that focus on a combination of performance measures and process measures. Performance measures are commonly used and relatively straightforward to measure. Performance measures generally include observable actions such as whether medics choose appropriate treatments at the right time and implement them effectively, or if military leaders choose effective tactics and communicate them effectively. Process measures are used less frequently, but provide important insight into whether learners are attending to relevant cues, accurately interpreting cues to make sense of the situation, and are able to mentally simulate potential interventions and outcomes to evaluate actions before they are implemented. These types of measures are tailored to each evaluation scenario. Often, experienced practitioners are asked to participate in training scenarios and an expert model is developed based on the cues the experts attend to, the meaning they make from the situation, and the opportunities and pitfalls they identify using mental simulation. Designing strategies to effectively assess recognition skills requires careful design and close collaboration with skilled practitioners. Assessing the impact of training on skill retention, on-the-job performance, and real-world outcomes such as fewer accidents or more lives saved is even more challenging – sometimes referred to as the holy grail of training evaluation.

Despite these challenges, augmented reality training applications are in use today and many others are being developed. We anticipate that the hardware platforms for augmented reality will become increasingly available, affordable, and powerful in the coming years. As increased processing power becomes available on augmented reality platforms, training designers will have even more scope for creating training applications. For example, more processing power would enable even higher visual fidelity. Designers could incorporate external sensor data to track learner movements and interactions with physical objects. Training simulation could leverage natural language processing to create enhanced interactions with virtual patients and avatars. Integrating artificial intelligence technologies would become feasible, opening the door to incorporating intelligent tutoring components to assess learner needs in real time and introduce or withdraw scaffolding as the scenario unfolds. We look forward to continuing innovation as augmented reality technology matures.

References

Air Force Manual. (2003). *Guidebook for Air Force Instructors* (36–2236). www
.angtec.ang.af.mil/Portals/10/Courses%20resources/afman36-2236.pdf?ver=
2018–10-02–084122-.

Allen, L. K., Mills, C., Jacovina, M. E., Crossley, S., D'Mello, S., & McNamara, D. S.
(2016). Investigating boredom and engagement during writing using multiple
sources of information: The essay, the writer, and keystrokes. Proceedings of the
Sixth International Conference on Learning Analytics & Knowledge, USA,
114–123. https://doi.org/10.1145/2883851.2883939.

Arai, S. M. (1997). Empowerment: From the theoretical to the personal. *Journal of
Leisurability, 24*(1), 3–11.

Arnone, M. P. (2003). *Using instructional design strategies to foster curiosity
(ED479842)*. ERIC. https://eric.ed.gov/?q=ED479842&id=ED479842.

Bathalon, S., Dorion, D., Darveau, S., & Martin, M. (2005). Cognitive skills
analysis, kinesiology, and mental imagery in the acquisition of surgical skills.
Journal of Otolaryngology, 34(5), 328–332. https://doi.org/10.2310/7070
.2005.34506.

Benner, P. (1984). From novice to expert: Excellence and power in clinical nursing
practice. *The American Journal of Nursing, 84*(12), 1480. https://doi.org/10.1097
/00000446-198412000-00025.

Bloom, B. S. (ed.), Engelhart, M. D., Furst, E. J., Hill, W. H., & Krathwohl, D. R.
(1956). *Taxonomy of educational objectives: The classification of educational goals.
Handbook 1: Cognitive domain.* Longman.

Boud, D., & Walker, D. (1998). Promoting reflection in professional courses: The
challenge of context. *Studies in Higher Education, 23*(2), 191–206. https://doi.org
/10.1080/03075079812331380384.

Brown, B. L. (1997). *New learning strategies for generation X* (ED411414). ERIC.
http://files.eric.ed.gov/fulltext/ED411414.pdf.

Brown, E., & Cairns, P. (2004). A grounded investigation of game immersion.
Proceedings of the International Conference on Human Factors in Computing
Systems, Austria, 1297–1300. https://doi.org/10.1145/985921.986048.

Brown, J. S., Collins, A., & Duguid, P. (1989). Situated cognition and the culture of
learning. *Educational Researcher, 18*(1), 32–42. https://doi.org/10.3102
/0013189X018001032.

Bulger, M. E., Mayer, R. E., Almeroth, K. C., & Blau, S. D. (2008). Measuring learner engagement in computer-equipped college classrooms. *Journal of Educational Multimedia and Hypermedia, 17*(2), 129–143.

Burroughs, W. A. (1984). Visual simulation training of baseball batters. *International Journal of Sport Psychology, 15*(2), 117–126.

Butler, F. K. (2017). TCCC updates: Two decades of saving lives on the battlefield: Tactical combat casualty care turns 20. *Journal of Special Operations Medicine: A Peer Reviewed Journal for SOF Medical Professionals, 17*(2), 166–172.

Carroll, J. (2014). Creating minimalist instruction. *International Journal of Designs for Learning, 5*(2), 56–65. https://doi.org/10.14434/ijdl.v5i2.12887.

Chase, W. G., & Simon, H. A. (1973a). Perception in chess. *Cognitive Psychology, 4* (1), 55–81. https://doi.org/10.1016/0010-0285(73)90004-2.

Chase, W. G., & Simon, H. A. (1973b). The mind's eye in chess. Proceedings of the Eighth Annual Carnegie Symposium on Cognition, USA, 215–281. https://doi.org/10.1016/B978-0-12-170150-5.50011-1.

Cheng, M.-T., She, H.-C., & Annetta, L. A. (2015). Game immersion experience: Its hierarchical structure and impact on game-based science learning. *Journal of Computer Assisted Learning, 31*(3), 232–253. https://doi.org/10.1111/j cal.12066.

Chi, M. T. H., Bassok, M., Lewis, M. W., Reimann, P., & Glaser, R. (1989). Self-explanations: How students study and use examples in learning to solve problems. *Cognitive Science, 13*(2), 145–182. https://doi.org/10.1016/0364-0213(89)90002-5.

Chi, M. T. H., De Leeuw, N., Chiu, M.-H., & LaVancher, C. (1994). Eliciting self-explanations improves understanding. *Cognitive Science, 18*(3), 439–477. https://doi.org/10.1016/0364-0213(94)90016-7.

Cohen, E. R., Barsuk, J. H., Moazed, F., Caprio, T., Didwania, A., McGaghie, W. C., & Wayne, D. B. (2013). Making July safer: Simulation-based mastery learning during intern boot camp. *Academic Medicine, 88*(2), 233–239. https://doi.org/10 .1097/acm.0b013e31827bfc0a.

Cohen, M. S., Thompson, B. B., Adelman, L., Bresnick, T. A., Shastri, L., & Riedel, S. L. (2000). *Training critical thinking for the battlefield* (Report No. ADA320892). Cognitive Technologies. https://apps.dtic.mil/sti/pdfs/AD A320892.pdf.

Collins, J. W., & O'Brien, N. P. (eds.) (2003). *The Greenwood dictionary of education.* Greenwood Press.

Cook, T. M., Green, C., McGrath, J., & Srivastava, R. (2007). Evaluation of four airway training manikins as patient simulators for the insertion of single use laryngeal mask airways. *Anaesthesia, 62*(7), 713–718. https://doi.org/10.1111/j.1365 -2044.2007.05068.x.

Crandall, B., & Getchell-Reiter, K. (1993). Critical decision method: A technique for eliciting concrete assessment indicators from the intuition of NICU nurses. *Advances in Nursing Science, 16*(1), 42–51. https://doi.org/10.1097/00012272-19 9309000-00006.

Crandall, B., Klein, G., & Hoffman, R. R. (2006). *Working minds: A practitioner's guide to cognitive task analysis.* MIT Press.

Csikszentmihalyi, M., Abuhamdeh, S., & Nakamura, J. (2014). Flow. In *Flow and the foundations of positive psychology* (pp. 227–238). Springer, Dordrecht. https:// doi.org/10.1007/978-94-017-9088-8_15.

D'Mello, S., Dieterle, E., & Duckworth, A. (2017). Advanced, analytic, automated (AAA) measurement of engagement during learning. *Educational Psychologist, 52*(2), 104–123. https://doi.org/10.1080/00461520.2017.1281747.

Devereux, L., & Wilson, K. (2008). Scaffolding literacies across the Bachelor of Education program: An argument for a course-wide approach. *Asia-Pacific Journal of Teacher Education, 36*(2), 121–134. https://doi.org/10.1080 /13598660801971633.

Dewey, J. (1933). *How we think*. Prometheus Books.

DiBello, L. (December, 2018). *Accelerating Expertise; we really outdid ourselves this time*. [Post]. LinkedIn. www.linkedin.com/pulse/accelerating-expertise-we-really-outdid-ourselves-time-lia-dibello/.

Dirkx, J. M. (2001). The power of feelings: Emotion, imagination, and the construction of meaning in adult learning. *New Directions for Adult and Continuing Education*, 2001(89), 63–72. https://doi.org/10.1002/ace.9.

Dreyfus, S. E., & Dreyfus, H. L. (1980). *A five-stage model of the mental activities involved in directed skill acquisition* (Report No. ADA084551). California Univ. Berkeley Operations Research Center. https://apps.dtic.mil/sti/pdfs/AD A084551.pdf.

Driskell, J. E., Copper, C., & Moran, A. (1994). Does mental practice enhance performance? *Journal of Applied Psychology, 79*(4), 481. https://doi.org/10.1037 /0021-9010.79.4.481.

Driver, R., Asojo, R., Leach, J., Mortimer, E., & Scott, P. (1994). Constructing scientific knowledge in the classroom. *Educational Researcher, 23*(7), 5–12. https:// doi.org/10.3102/0013189X023007005.

Dror, I. (2011). A novel approach to minimize error in the medical domain: Cognitive neuroscientific insights into training. *Medical Teacher, 33*(1), 34–38. https://doi.org/10.3109/0142159X.2011.535047.

Dweck, C. S., & Leggett, E. L. (1988). A social-cognitive approach to motivation and personality. *Psychological Review, 95*(2), 256–273. https://doi.org/10.1037/0 033-295X.95.2.256.

Earley, C., Northcraft, G., Lee, C., & Lituchy, T. (1990). Impact of process and outcome feedback on the relation of goal setting to task performance. *Academy of Management Journal, 33*(1), 87–105. https://doi.org/10.5465/256353.

Einhorn, H. J. (1974). Expert judgment: Some necessary conditions and an example. *Journal of Applied Psychology, 59*(5), 562.

Einhorn, H. J., & Hogarth, R. M. (1981). Behavioral decision theory: Processes of judgement and choice. *Annual Review of Psychology, 32*(1), 53–88. https://doi.org /10.1037/h0037164.

Engelbrecht, L., Terblanche, E., & Welman, K. E. (2016). Video-based perceptual training as a method to improve reactive agility performance in rugby union players. *International Journal of Sports Science & Coaching, 11*(6), 799–809. https:// doi.org/10.1177/1747954116676106.

Eppler, M. A., & Harju, B. J. (1997). Achievement motivation goals in relation to academic performance in traditional and non-traditional college students. *Research in Higher Education*, *38*, 557–573. https://doi.org/10.1023/A:1024944429347.

Ericsson, K. A. (2004). Deliberate practice and the acquisition and maintenance of expert performance in medicine and related domains. *Academic Medicine*, *79* (10), 70–81. https://doi.org/10.1097/00001888-200410001-00022.

Ericsson, K. A., Charness, N., Feltovich, P. J., & Hoffman, R. R. (2006). *The Cambridge handbook of expertise and expert performance*. Cambridge University Press.

Ericsson, K. A., Krampe, R. T., & Tesch-Römer, C. (1993). The role of deliberate practice in the acquisition of expert performance. *Psychological Review*, *100*(3), 363–406. https://doi.org/10.1037/0033-295X.100.3.363.

Esteban-Millat, I., Martínez-López, F. J., Huertas-García, R., Meseguer, A., & Rodríguez-Ardura, I. (2014). Modelling students' flow experiences in an online learning environment. *Computers and Education*, *71*, 111–123. https://doi.org/10.1016/j.compedu.2013.09.012.

Fadde, P. J. (2006). Interactive video training of perceptual decision-making in the sport of baseball. *Technology, Instruction, Cognition and Learning*, *4*(3), 265–285.

Fadde, P. J. (2007). Seeing is believing: Video mock-ups to evaluate and demonstrate multimedia designs. *TechTrends*, *51*(4), 32–38. https://doi.org/10.1007/s11528-007-0053-5.

Fadde, P. J. (2009). Instructional design for advanced learners: Training recognition skills to hasten expertise. *Educational Technology Research and Development*, *57*(3), 359–376. https://doi.org/10.1007/s11423-007-9046-5.

Fadde, P. J., & Klein, G. A. (2010). Deliberate performance: Accelerating expertise in natural settings. *Performance Improvement*, *49*(9), 5–14. https://doi.org/10.1002/pfi.20175.

Farrow, D., Chivers, P., Hardingham, C., & Sacshse, S. (1998). The effect of video-based perceptual training on the tennis return of serve. *International Journal of Sport Psychology*, *29*(3), 231–242.

Fiore, S. M., Cuevas, H. M., & Oser, R. L. (2003). A picture is worth a thousand connections: The facilitative effects of diagrams on mental model development and task performance. *Computers in Human Behavior*, *19*(2), 185–199. https://doi.org/10.1016/S0747-5632(02)00054-7.

Fiore, S. M., Hoffman, R. R., & Salas, E. (2008). Learning and performance across disciplines: An epilogue for moving multidisciplinary research toward an interdisciplinary science of expertise. *Military Psychology*, *20* (sup1), S155–S170. https://doi.org/10.1080/08995600701804939.

Geis, G. L., Wheeler, D. S., Bunger, A., Militello, L. G., Taylor, R. G., Bauer, J. P., Byczkowski, T. L., Kerry, B. T., & Patterson, M. D. (2018). A validation argument for a simulation-based training course centered on assessment, recognition, and early management of pediatric sepsis. *Simulation in Healthcare*, *13*(1), 16–26. https://doi.org/10.1097/SIH.0000000000000271.

Ghani, J. A., & Deshpande, S. P. (1994). Task characteristics and the experience of optimal flow in human-computer interaction. *The Journal of Psychology, 128*(4), 381–391. https://doi.org/10.1080/00223980.1994.9712742.

Gibson, E. J. (1969). *Principles of perceptual learning and development.* Prentice-Hall.

Gibson, E. J. (2000). Perceptual learning in development: Some basic concepts. *Ecological Psychology, 12*(4), 295–302. https://doi.org/10.1207/S15326969 ECO1204_04.

Gibson, J. J. (1958). Visually controlled locomotion and visual orientation in animals. *British Journal of Psychology, 49*(3), 182–194. https://doi.org/10.1111/j .2044-8295.1958.tb00656.x.

Goldberg, L. R. (1968). Simple models or simple processes? Some research on clinical judgments. *American Psychologist, 23*(7), 483–496. https://doi.org/10 .1037/h0026206.

Goldstone, R. L., & Barsalou, L. W. (1998). Reuniting perception and conception. *Cognition, 65*(2–3), 231–262. https://doi.org/10.1016/S0010-0277(97)00047-4.

Gorini, A., Capideville, C. S., De Leo, G., Mantovani, F., & Riva, G. (2011). The role of immersion and narrative in mediated presence: The virtual hospital experience. *Cyberpsychology, Behavior, and Social Networking, 14*(3), 99–105. https://doi.org/10 .1089/cyber.2010.0100.

Gorman, J., Cooke, N., & Amazeen, P. (2010). Training adaptive teams. *Human Factors, 52,* 295–307. https://doi.org/10.1177/0018720810371689.

Grabinger, R. S. (1996). Rich environments for active learning. In D. H. Jonassen (ed.), *Handbook of research for educational communications and technology* (pp. 665–692). Macmillan.

Halverson, L. R., & Graham, C. R. (2019). Learner engagement in blended learning environments: A conceptual framework. *Online Learning, 23*(2), 145–178. http://dx.doi.org/10.24059/olj.v23i2.1481.

Hatton, N., & Smith, D. (1995). Reflection in teacher education: Towards definition and implementation. *Teaching and Teacher Education, 11*(1), 33–49. https://doi.org/10.1016/0742-051X(94)00012-U.

Hays, R. T., & Singer, M. J. (2012). *Simulation fidelity in training system design: Bridging the gap between reality and training.* Springer. https://doi.org/10.1007 /978-1-4612-3564-4.

Healy, A. F. (2007). Transfer: Specificity and generality. In H. L. Roediger, Y. Dudai, & S. M. Fitzpatrick (eds.), *Science of memory: Concepts* (pp. 271–275). Oxford University Press. https://doi.org/10.1093/acprof:oso/9780195310443.001.0001

Heeter, C. (1992). Being there: The subjective experience of presence. *Presence Teleoperators and Virtual Environments, 1*(2), 262–271. https://doi.org/10.1162/ pres.1992.1.2.262.

Hernandez, O. (2021). Designing simulation-based active learning activities using augmented reality and sets of offline games. [Unpublished doctoral dissertation].The Ohio State University.

Hoffman, P. J., Slovic, P., & Rorer, L. G. (1968). An analysis-of-variance model for the assessment of configural cue utilization in clinical judgment. *Psychological Bulletin, 69*(5), 338–349. https://doi.org/10.1037/h0025665.

Hoffman, R., Feltovich, P., Fiore, S., Klein, G., Missildine, W., & DiBello, L. (2010). *Accelerated proficiency and facilitated retention: Recommendations based on an integration of research and findings from a working meeting* (Report No. ADA536308). Florida Institute for Human and Machine Cognition. https://a pps.dtic.mil/sti/pdfs/ADA536308.pdf.

Hoffman, R. R., & Militello, L. G. (2008). *Perspectives on cognitive task analysis: Historical origins and modern communities of practice*. Psychology Press.

Hoffman, R. R., Ward, P., Feltovich, P. J., DiBello, L., Fiore, S. M., & Andrews, D. H. (2013). *Accelerated expertise: Training for high proficiency in a complex world*. Psychology Press.

Hogarth, R. M. (2001). *Educating intuition*. University of Chicago Press. https://doi.org/10.1080/00223980.1994.9712742.

Hu, Y.-Y., Peyre, S. E., Arriaga, A. F., Roth, E. M., Corso, K. A., & Greenberg, C. C. (2012). War stories: A qualitative analysis of narrative teaching strategies in the operating room. *The American Journal of Surgery, 203*(1), 63–68. https://doi.org/10.1016/j.amjsurg.2011.08.005.

Hunt, E. A., Duval-Arnould, J. M., Nelson-McMillan, K. L., Bradshaw, J. H., Diener-West, M., Perretta, J. S., & Shilkofski, N. A. (2014). Pediatric resident resuscitation skills improve after "Rapid Cycle Deliberate Practice" training. *Resuscitation, 85*(7), 945–951. https://doi.org/10.1016/j.resuscitation.2014.02.025.

Isen, A. M. (2000). Positive affect and decision making. In M. Lewis, & J. M. Haviland (eds.), *Handbook of emotions* (pp. 261–277). Guilford Press.

Jackson, K. M., & Cook, T. M. (2007). Evaluation of four airway training manikins as patient simulators for the insertion of eight types of supraglottic airway devices. *Anaesthesia, 62*(4), 388–393. https://doi.org/10.1111/j.1365-2044.2007.04983.x.

Jean, L., & Wenger, E. (1991). *Situated learning: Legitimate peripheral participation*. Cambridge University Press.

Jensen, R., Nolan, M., Harmon, N., & Caldwell, G. (2006). *Visually based timeline debrief toolset for team training AAR* (Report No. ADA457460). Stottler Henke Associates. https://apps.dtic.mil/sti/pdfs/ADA457460.pdf.

Kahneman, D. (2011). *Thinking fast and slow*. Farrar, Straus and Giroux.

Kahneman, D., & Klein, G. (2009). Conditions for intuitive expertise: A failure to disagree. *American Psychologist, 64*(6), 515–526. https://doi.org/10.1037/a0016755.

Kahneman, D., & Tversky, A. (1982). The simulation heuristic. In D. Kahneman, P. Slovic, & A. Tversky (eds.), *Judgment under uncertainty: Heuristics and biases* (pp. 201–208). Cambridge University Press.

Keith, N., & Frese, M. (2008). Effectiveness of error management training: A meta-analysis. *Journal of Applied Psychology, 93*(1), 59–69. https://doi.org/10.1037/0021-9010.93.1.59.

Kellman, P. J. (2002). Perceptual learning. In H. Pashler, & R. Gallistel (eds.), *Stevens' handbook of experimental psychology: Learning, motivation, and emotion* (pp. 259–299). Wiley & Sons. https://doi.org/10.1002/0471214426.pas0307.

Kellman, P. J., & Garrigan, P. (2009). Perceptual learning and human expertise. *Physics of Life Reviews, 6*(2), 53–84. https://doi.org/10.1080/0142159X.2018.1484897.

Kellman, P. J., & Krasne, S. (2018). Accelerating expertise: Perceptual and adaptive learning technology in medical learning. *Medical Teacher, 40*(8), 797–802. https://doi.org/10.1080/0142159X.2018.1484897.

Kidman, L., Thorpe, R., Jones, R. L., & Lewis, C. (2001). *Developing decision makers: An empowerment approach to coaching.* Innovative Print Communications.

Kim, J. M., Hill Jr, R. W., Durlach, P. J., Lane, H. C., Forbell, E., Core, M., Marsella, S., Pynadath, D., & Hart, J. (2009). BiLAT: A game-based environment for practicing negotiation in a cultural context. *International Journal of Artificial Intelligence in Education, 19*(3), 289–308.

Klasen, J. M., & Lingard, L. A. (2019). Allowing failure for educational purposes in postgraduate clinical training: a narrative review. *Medical Teacher, 41*(11), 1263–1269. https://doi.org/10.1080/0142159X.2019.1630728.

Klein, D. E., Klein, H. A., & Klein, G. (2000). Macrocognition: Linking cognitive psychology and cognitive ergonomics. *Proceedings of the Fifth International Conference on Human Interactions with Complex Systems,* 173–177.

Klein, G. (1998). *Sources of power: How people make decisions.* MIT Press.

Klein, G., & Borders, J. (2016). The ShadowBox approach to cognitive skills training: An empirical evaluation. *Journal of Cognitive Engineering and Decision Making, 10*(3), 268–280. https://doi.org/10.1177/1555343416636515.

Klein, G., Calderwood, R., & Clinton-Cirocco, A. (1988). *Rapid decision making on the fire ground* (Report No. ADA199492). Klein Associates. https://apps.dtic.mil/sti/pdfs/ADA199492.pdf.

Klein, G., Calderwood, R., & Clinton-Cirocco, A. (2010). Rapid decision making on the fire ground: The original study plus a postscript. *Journal of Cognitive Engineering and Decision Making, 4*(3), 186–209. https://doi.org/10.1518/155534310X12844000801203.

Klein, G., & Crandall, B. W. (1995). The role of mental simulation in problem solving and decision making. In P. A. Hancock, J. M. Flach, J. Caird, & K. J. Vicente (eds.), *Local applications of the ecological approach to human-machine systems* (pp. 324–358). CRC Press.

Klein, G., & Hoffman, R. R. (2008). Macrocognition, mental models, and cognitive task analysis methodology. In J. M. Schraagen, L. G. Millitello, T. Ormerod, & R. Lipshitz (eds.), *Naturalistic decision making and macrocognition* (pp. 57–80). Ashgate.

Klein, G., Moon, B., & Hoffman, R. R. (2006a). Making sense of sensemaking 1: Alternative perspectives. *IEEE Intelligent Systems, 21*(1), 70–73. https://doi.org/10.1109/MIS.2006.75.

Klein, G., Moon, B., & Hoffman, R. R. (2006b). Making sense of sensemaking 2: A macrocognitive model. *IEEE Intelligent Systems, 21*(5), 88–92. https://doi.org/10.1109/MIS.2006.100.

Klein, G., Pliske, R., Crandall, B., & Woods, D. D. (2005). Problem detection. *Cognition, Technology & Work, 7*(1), 14–28. https://doi.org/10.1007/s10111-004-0166-y.

Klein, G., Ross, K. G., Moon, B. M., Klein, D. E., Hoffman, R. R., & Hollnagel, E. (2003). Macrocognition. *IEEE Intelligent Systems, 18*(3), 81–85. https://doi.org/10.1109/MIS.2003.1200735.

Kolb, D. A. (1975). Toward an applied theory of experiential learning. In C. Cooper (ed.), *Studies of group process* (pp. 33–57). Wiley.

Larkin, P., Mesagno, C., Berry, J., & Spittle, M. (2018). Exploration of the perceptual-cognitive processes that contribute to in-game decision-making of Australian football umpires. *International Journal of Sport and Exercise Psychology, 16*(2), 112–124. https://doi.org/10.1080/1612197X.2016.1167760.

Lauber, B., & Keller, M. (2014). Improving motor performance: Selected aspects of augmented feedback in exercise and health. *European Journal of Sport Science, 14*(1), 36–43. https://doi.org/10.1080/17461391.2012.725104.

Lillis, T. M. (2001). *Student writing: Access, regulation, desire.* Psychology Press.

Lindsley, D. H., Daniel J. B., & James B. T. (1995). Efficacy-performing spirals: A multilevel perspective. *Academy of Management Review, 20*(3), 645–678. https://doi.org/10.5465/amr.1995.9508080333.

Lintern, G., & Boot, W. R. (2021). Cognitive training: Transfer beyond the laboratory. *Human Factors, 63*(3), 531–547. https://doi.org/10.1177/0018720819879814.

Lintern, G., Taylor, H. L., Koonce, J. M., Kaiser, R. H., & Morrison, G. A. (1997). Transfer and quasi-transfer effects of scene detail and visual augmentation in landing training. *The International Journal of Aviation Psychology, 7*(2), 149–169. https://doi.org/10.1207/s15327108ijap0702_4.

Loughran, J. J. (2002). *Developing reflective practice: Learning about teaching and learning through modelling.* Routledge.

Luckin, R., & Du Boulay, B. (1999). Ecolab: The development and evaluation of a Vygotskian design framework. *International Journal of Artificial Intelligence in Education, 10*(2), 198–220.

MacMahon, C., Helsen, W. F., Starkes, J. L., & Weston, M. (2007). Decision-making skills and deliberate practice in elite association football referees. *Journal of Sports Sciences, 25*(1), 65–78. https://doi.org/10.1080/02640410600718640.

Mann, D. T., Williams, A. M., Ward, P., & Janelle, C. M. (2007). Perceptual-cognitive expertise in sport: A meta-analysis. *Journal of Sport and Exercise Psychology, 29*(4), 457–478. https://doi.org/10.1123/jsep.29.4.457.

Mariani, L. (1997). Teacher support and teacher challenge in promoting learner autonomy. *Perspectives, 23*(2), 5–19.

Mayer, R. E. (2003). *Learning and instruction.* Prentice Hall.

Mayer, R. E. (ed.). (2005). *The Cambridge handbook of multimedia learning.* Cambridge University Press.

McLeod, S. A. (2017, Oct 24). *Kolb-learning styles.* Simply Psychology. www.simplypsychology.org/learning-kolb.html.

Merrill, D. (2002). First principals of instruction. *Educational Technology Research and Development, 50*(3), 43–59. https://doi.org/10.1007/BF02505024.

Michael, J. (2006). Where's the evidence that active learning works? *Advances in physiology education. 30*(4), 159–167. https://doi.org/10.1152/advan.00053.2006.

Mikulincer, M. (1989). Cognitive interference and learned helplessness: The effects of off-task cognitions on performance following unsolvable problems. *Journal of Personality and Social Psychology, 57*(1), 129–135. https://doi.org/10.1037/0022-3514.57.1.129.

Militello, L. G., & Hoffman, R. R. (2008). The forgotten history of cognitive task analysis. *Proceedings of the Human Factors and Ergonomics Society Annual Meeting, 52*(4), 383–387. https://doi.org/10.1177/154193120805200439.

Militello, L. G., & Hutton, R. J. B. (1998). Applied cognitive task analysis (ACTA): A practitioner's toolkit for understanding cognitive task demands. *Ergonomics, 41*(11), 1618–1641. https://doi.org/10.1080/001401398186108.

Militello, L. G., Hutton, R. J. B., Pliske, R. M., Knight, B. J., & Klein, G. (1997). *Applied Cognitive Task Analysis (ACTA) methodology* (Report. No. ADA335225). Klein Associates. https://apps.dtic.mil/sti/pdfs/ADA335225.pdf.

Militello, L. G., & Lim, L. (1995). Patient assessment skills: Assessing early cues of necrotizing enterocolitis. *Journal of Perinatal and Neonatal Nursing, 9*(2), 42–52. https://doi.org/10.1097/00005237-199509000-00007.

Militello, L. G., Roth, E. M., Scheff, S., Ernst, K. M., Susshereba, C. E., Diiulio, J. B., & Klein, D. E. (2019). Toward an optimally crewed future vertical lift vehicle: Crewing strategies and recommendations (unpublished technical report, Contract No. NNX16AJ91A, 21-1614-5637 – ADS2018). Dayton, Ohio.

Militello, L. G., Susshereba, C., Wolf, S., & Fernandez, R. (2021). Developing a just-in-time refresher trainer for advanced life support in austere regions: Phase I final report (unpublished technical report, Contract No. W81XWH21P0013). Dayton, OH.

Miller, J. E., & Patterson, E. S. (2018). *Macrocognition metrics and scenarios: Design and evaluation for real-world teams.* CRC Press.

Nash, E. B., Edwards, G. W., Thompson, J. A., & Barfield, W. (2000). A review of presence and performance in virtual environments. *International Journal of Human-Computer Interaction, 12*(1), 1–41. https://doi.org/10.1207/S15327590IJHC1201_1.

Newsome, E., Militello, L. G., & Ramachandran, S. (2020). Stratagems: Embedding cognitive training in game-based environments. *Proceedings of the International Conference on Applied Human Factors and Ergonomics*, USA, *1217*, 589–595. https://doi.org/10.1007/978-3-030-51828-8_77.

Nguyen, Q. D., Fernandez, N., Karsenti, T., & Charlin, B. (2014). What is reflection? A conceptual analysis of major definitions and a proposal of a five-component model. *Medical Education, 48*(12), 1176–1189. https://doi.org/10.1111/medu.12583.

Norman, D. A. (2013). *The design of everyday things: Revised and expanded edition.* Basic Books.

Norman, D. A. (1986). User centered system design. In D. A. Norman, & S. W. Draper (eds.), *Cognitive engineering* (pp. 31–61). Lawrence Erlbaum Associates.

Novak, J. D., & Gowin, D. B. (1984). *Learning how to learn.* Cambridge University Press.

Odetola, F. O., Rosenberg, A. L., Davis, M. M., Clark, S. J., Dechert, R. E., & Shanley, T. P. (2008). Do outcomes vary according to the source of admission to the pediatric intensive care unit? *Pediatric Critical Care Medicine, 9*(1), 20–25. https://doi.org/10.1097/01.pcc.0000298642.11872.29.

Patterson, E. S., & Hoffman, R. R. (2012). Visualization framework of macro-cognition functions. *Cognition, Technology & Work, 14*(3), 221–227. https://doi.org/10.1007/s10111-011-0208-1.

Patterson, M. D., Militello, L. G., Bunger, A., Taylor, R. G., Wheeler, D. S., Klein, G., & Geis, G. L. (2016). Leveraging the critical decision method to develop simulation-based training for early recognition of sepsis. *Journal of Cognitive Engineering and Decision Making, 10*(1), 36–56. https://doi.org/10.1177/1555343416629520.

Patterson, R. E., Pierce, B. J., Bell, H. H., & Klein, G. (2010). Implicit learning, tacit knowledge, expertise development, and naturalistic decision making. *Journal of Cognitive Engineering and Decision Making, 4*(4), 289–303. https://doi.org/10.1177/155534341000400403.

Pearce, J. M., Ainley, M., & Howard, S. (2005). The ebb and flow of online learning. *Computers in Human Behavior, 21*(55), 745–771. https://doi.org/10.1016/j.chb.2004.02.019.

Pekrun, R. (2011). Emotions as drivers of learning and cognitive development. In R. A. Calvo, & S. K. D'Mello (eds.), *New perspectives on affect and learning technologies* (pp. 23–39). Springer. https://doi.org/10.1007/978-1-4419-9625-1_3.

Petrov, A. A., Dosher, B. A., & Lu, Z.-L. (2005). The dynamics of perceptual learning: An incremental reweighting model. *Psychological Review, 112*(4), 715–743. https://doi.org/10.1037/0033-295X.112.4.715.

Picard, R. W., Papert, S., Bender, W., Blumberg, B., Breazeal, C., Cavallo, D., Machover, T., Resnick, M., Roy, D., & Strohecker, C. (2004). Affective learning – A manifesto. *BT Technology Journal, 22*(4), 253–269. https://doi.org/10.1023/B:BTTJ.0000047603.37042.33.

Polanyi, M. (1966). Tacit Dimension. In L. Prusak (ed.), *Knowledge in organizations* (pp. 135–147). Routledge.

Price, M., Handley, K., Millar, J., & O'Donovan, B. (2010). Feedback: All that effort, but what is the effect? *Assessment & Evaluation in Higher Education, 35*(3), 277–289. https://doi.org/10.1080/02602930903541007.

Psotka, J. (1995). Immersive training systems: Virtual reality and education and training. *Instructional Science, 23*(5), 405–431. https://doi.org/10.1007/BF00896880.

Ramachandran, S., Domeshek, E. A., Jensen, R., & Aukamp, A. (2016). Uncovering the hidden: Tradeoffs in rationale elicitation for situated tutors. Proceedings of the Interservice/Industry Training, Simulation, and Education Conference. USA.

Richards, P. (2005). Empowering the decision-making process in the competitive sport environment through using reflective practice. Can performance intelligence be taught [Paper Presentation]. Fourth Carfax International Conference on Reflective Practice, USA.

Richards, P., Mascarenhas, D. R. D., & Collins, D. (2009). Implementing reflective practice approaches with elite team athletes: Parameters of success. *Reflective Practice, 10*(3), 353–363. https://doi.org/10.1080/14623940903034721.

Robson, S., & Manacapilli, T. (2014). *Enhancing performance under stress: Stress inoculation training for battlefield airmen* (Report No. ADA605157). RAND PROJECT AIR FORCE. https://apps.dtic.mil/sti/pdfs/ADA605157.pdf.

Ross, S. L. (1985). The effectiveness of mental practice in improving the performance of college trombonists. *Journal of Research in Music Education, 33*(4), 221–230. https://doi.org/10.2307/3345249.

Rouse, W. B., & Morris, N. M. (1986). On looking into the black box: Prospects and limits in the search for mental models. *Psychological Bulletin, 100*(3), 349–363. https://doi.org/10.1037/0033-2909.100.3.349.

Roza, Z. C. (2004). *Simulation Fidelity Theory and Practice: A unified approach to defining, specifying, and measuring the realism of simulations.* [Doctoral thesis, Delft University] DUP Science: Delft.

Sackett, R. S. (1934). The influence of symbolic rehearsal upon the retention of a maze habit. *The Journal of General Psychology, 10*(2), 376–398. https://doi.org/10.1080/00221309.1934.9917742.

Sackett, R. S. (1935). The relationship between amount of symbolic rehearsal and retention of a maze habit. *The Journal of General Psychology, 13*(1), 113–130. https://doi.org/10.1080/00221309.1935.9917869.

Salas, E., Cannon-Bowers, J. A., Fiore, S. M., & Stout, R. J. (2001). Cue-recognition training to enhance team situational awareness. In M. McNeese, E. Salas, & M. Endsley (eds.), *New trends in cooperative activities: Understanding system dynamics in complex environments* (pp. 169–190). Human Factors and Ergonomics Society.

San Pedro, M. O. Z., Baker, R. S. J. d., Gowda, S. M., & Heffernan, N. T. (2013). Towards an understanding of affect and knowledge from student interaction with an intelligent tutoring system. *Proceedings of the International Conference on Artificial Intelligence in Education, 7926*, 41–50. https://doi.org/10.1007/978-3-642-39112-5_5.

Sanders, C. W., Sadoski, M., Wasserman, R. M., Wiprud, R., English, M., & Bramson, R. (2007). Comparing the effects of physical practice and mental imagery rehearsal on learning basic venipuncture by medical students. *Imagination, Cognition and Personality, 27*(2), 117–127. https://doi.org/10.2190/IC.27.2.c.

Schebesta, K., Hüpfl, M., Roessler, B., Ringl, H., Mueller, M. P., & Kimberger, O. (2012). Degrees of reality: Airway anatomy of high-fidelity human patient simulators and airway trainers. *Anesthesiology: The Journal of the American Society of Anesthesiologists, 116*(6), 1204–1209. https://doi.org/10.1097/ALN.0b013e318254cf41.

Schön, D. A. (1987). *Educating the reflective practitioner: Toward a new design for teaching and learning in the professions.* Jossey-Bass.

Schraagen, J. M., Militello, L. G., Ormerod, T., & Lipshitz, R. (eds.). (2008). *Naturalistic decision making and acrocognition.* Ashgate.

Schworm, S., & Renkl, A. (2006). Computer-supported example-based learning: When instructional explanations reduce self-explanations. *Computers & Education, 46*(4), 426–445. https://doi.org/10.1016/j.compedu.2004.08.011.

Seel, N. M., & Dinter, F. R. (1995). Instruction and mental model progression: Learner-dependent effects of teaching strategies on knowledge acquisition and analogical transfer. *Educational Research and Evaluation, 1*(1), 4–35. https://doi.org/10.1080/1380361950010102.

Shanteau, J. (1992). How much information does an expert use? Is it relevant? *Acta Psychologica, 81*(1), 75–86. https://doi.org/10.1016/0001-6918(92)90012-3.

Sherman, W. R., & Craig, A. B. (2018). *Understanding virtual reality: Interface, application, and design* (2nd ed). Morgan Kaufmann.

Silsby, J., Jordan, G., Bayley, G., & Cook, T. M. (2006). Evaluation of four airway training manikins as simulators for inserting the LMA Classic™. *Anaesthesia, 61*(6), 576–579. https://doi.org/10.1111/j.1365-2044.2006.04643.x.

Singh, D., Kojima, T., Gurnaney, H., & Deutsch, E. S. (2020). Do fellows and faculty share the same perception of simulation fidelity? A pilot study. *Simulation in Healthcare, 15*(4), 266–270. https://doi.org/10.1097/sih.0000000000000454.

Slovic, P. (1969). Analyzing the expert judge: A descriptive study of a stockbroker's decision process. *Journal of Applied Psychology, 53*(4), 255–263. https://doi.org/10.1037/h0027773.

Stottler, R., Panichas, S., & San Mateo, C. A. (2006). A new generation of tactical action officer intelligent tutoring system (ITS). Proceedings of Industry/Interservice, Training, Simulation and Education Conference, USA.

Sushereba, C. E., Militello, L. G., Wolf, S., & Patterson, E. S. (2021). Use of augmented reality to train sensemaking in high-stakes medical environments. *Journal of Cognitive Engineering and Decision Making, 15*(2–3), 55–65. https://doi.org/10.1177/15553434211019234.

Timmermann, A. (2011). Supraglottic airways in difficult airway management: Successes, failures, use and misuse. *Anaesthesia, 66*, 45–56. https://doi.org/10.1111/j.1365-2044.2011.06934.x.

Verkuyl, M., Lapum, J. L., Hughes, M., McCulloch, T., Liu, L., Mastrilli, P., Romaniuk, D., & Betts, L. (2018). Virtual gaming simulation: Exploring self-debriefing, virtual debriefing, and in-person debriefing. *Clinical Simulation in Nursing, 20*, 7–14. https://doi.org/10.1016/j.ecns.2018.04.006.

Vovk, A., Wild, F., Guest, W., & Kuula, T. (2018). Simulator sickness in augmented reality training using the Microsoft HoloLens. *Proceedings of the 2018 CHI Conference on Human Factors in Computing Systems*, 1–9. https://doi.org/10.1145/3173574.3173783.

Vygotsky, L. S. (1978). *Mind in society: The development of higher psychological processes*. Harvard University Press.

Vygotsky, L. S. (1987). *Thinking and speech*. (N. Minick, Trans.). Plenum Press. (Original work published 1934.)

Wang, M., & Kang, M. (2006). Cybergogy for engaged learning: A framework for creating learner engagement through information and communication technology. In D. Hung, & M. S. Khine (eds.), *Engaged learning with emerging technologies* (pp. 225–253). Springer, Dordrecht. https://doi.org/10.1007/1-4020-3669-8_11.

Ward, P., Gore, J., Hutton, R., Conway, G. E., & Hoffman, R. R. (2018). Adaptive skill as the *conditio sine qua non* of expertise. *Journal of Applied Research in Memory and Cognition, 7*(1), 35-50. https://doi.org/10.1016/j.jarmac.2018.01.009.

Wass, R., Harland, T., & Mercer, A. (2011). Scaffolding critical thinking in the zone of proximal development. *Higher Education Research & Development, 30* (3), 317–328. https://doi.org/10.1080/07294360.2010.489237.

Waterworth, J. A., Waterworth, E. L., & Westling, J. (2002). *Presence as performance: The mystique of digital participation* [Paper Presentation]. Presence Fifth Annual International Workshop.

Whetzel, D. L. & McDaniel, M. A. (2009). Situational judgment tests: An overview of current research. *Human Resource Management Review, 19*(3), 188–202. https://doi.org/10.1016/j.hrmr.2009.03.007.

Wickens, C. D., Hutchins, S., Carolan, T., & Cumming, J. (2013). Effectiveness of part-task training and increasing-difficulty training strategies: A meta-analysis approach. *Human Factors, 55*(2), 461–470. https://doi.org/10.1177/0018720812451994.

Wiet, G. J., Stredney, D., Kerwin, T., Hittle, B., Fernandez, S. A., Abdel-Rasoul, M., & Welling, D. B. (2012). Virtual temporal bone dissection system: OSU virtual temporal bone system: Development and testing. *Laryngoscope, 122*(S1), S1–S12. https://doi.org/10.1002/lary.22499.

Wiet, G. J., Stredney, D., Sessanna, D., Bryan, J. A., Welling D. B., & Schmalbrock, P. (2002). Virtual temporal bone dissection: An interactive surgical simulator. *Otolaryngol – Head Neck Surg. 127*(1), 79–83. https://doi.org/10.1067/mhn.2002.126588.

Wiggins, M., & O'Hare, D. (2003). Weatherwise: Evaluation of a cue-based training approach for the recognition of deteriorating weather conditions during flight. *Human Factors, 45*(2), 337–345. https://doi.org/10.1518/hfes.45.2.337.27246.

Wilson, K., & Devereux, L. (2014). Scaffolding theory: High challenge, high support in Academic Language and Learning (ALL) contexts. *Journal of Academic Language and Learning, 8*(3), A91–A100.

Winner, J., & Millwater, T. L. (2019). Evaluating human patient simulation fidelity and effectiveness for combat-medical training. *Proceedings of the International Symposium on Human Factors and Ergonomics in Health Care, USA, 8*(1), 176–180. https://doi.org/10.1177/2327857919081043.

Witmer, B. G., & Singer, M. J. (1994). *Measuring presence in virtual environments* (Report No. ADA286183). Army Research Institute for the Behavioral and Social Sciences. https://apps.dtic.mil/sti/pdfs/ADA286183.pdf.

Witmer, B. G., & Singer, M. J. (1998). Measuring presence in virtual environments: A presence questionnaire. *Presence, 7*(3), 225–240. https://doi.org/10.1162/105474698565686.

Wofford, J. C., & Goodwin, V. L. (1990). Effects of feedback on cognitive processing and choice of decision style. *Journal of Applied Psychology, 75*(6), 603–612. https://doi.org/10.1037/0021-9010.75.6.603.

Woolf, B. P. (2008). *Building intelligent interactive tutors: Student-centered strategies for revolutionizing e-learning.* Morgan Kaufmann.

Wylie, R., & Chi, M. T. H. (2014). The self-explanation principle in multimedia learning. In R. E. Mayer (ed.), *The Cambridge handbook of multimedia learning* (pp. 413–432). Cambridge University Press.

Young, J. Q., Ranji, S. R., Wachter, R. M., Lee, C. M., Niehaus, B., & Auerbach, A. D. (2011). "July effect": Impact of the academic year-end changeover on patient outcomes: A systematic review. *Annals of Internal Medicine, 155* (5), 309–315. https://doi.org/10.7326/0003-4819-155-5-201109060-00354.

Zajonc, R. B. (1980). Feeling and thinking: Preferences need no inferences. *American Psychologist, 35*(1), 151–175. http://dx.doi.org/10.1037/0003-066X .35.2.151.

Zhang, C., Perkis, A., & Arndt, S. (2017). Spatial immersion versus emotional immersion, which is more immersive? *Proceedings of the Ninth International Conference on Quality of Multimedia Experience,* Germany. https://doi.org/10 .1109/QoMEX.2017.7965655.

Zhu, E., Hadadgar, A., Masiello, I., & Zary, N. (2014). Augmented reality in healthcare education: An integrative review. *PeerJ, 2,* e469. https://doi.org/10 .7717%2Fpeerj.469.

Index

perceptual discrimination, 35, 130
perceptual skills, 51, 55, 59, 70, 130
phone, 19, 57, 68
physicians, 12, 29, 54, 64, 85
physics, 78, 133
pilots, 10, 13, 23, 36, 40, 47, 55, 64, 71
Pokémon Go, 3
presence, 19, 24, 26, 129
problem detection, 34, 35, 36, 42
problem solving, 21, 28, 59, 122
progressive difficulty, 69
psychological safety, 29, 33
psychomotor skills, 70

radiology, 57, 86
rationale
    expert, 80, 83, 113, 124
    tracking, 96–97, 111
reading comprehension, 78
recognition-primed decision model, 9–10, 47, 60, 106
recognition skills, 25, 67, 106, 123, 128
    components, 10–15
    definition, 5
    measurement, 135
    training, 9, 57, 74
    transfer, 36
recording, 112
    audio, 80
    learner's view, 104, 114, 132, 133
    video, 56, 112
reflection, 77, 80, 123, 134
    active, 88, 117
    definition, 109
    team-based, 111
reflective tutor, 113

scaffolding
    adaptive, 107
scenarios
    text-based, 23, 80
self-explanation, 78–79
sensemaking, 21, 55, 59, 67, 74, 82
    data-frame model, 12–15, 42, 67, 106
serious game, 30, 65, 71
ShadowBox, 23, 80, 110–111
simulation, 78
situational judgment test, 113
skilled performance, 48, 70, 85, 129
soccer, 89
sports, 57, 70, 87, 110
standard operating procedures, 34, 45, 84
Stratagems trainer, 23, 71
stress inoculation training, 21

tablet, 3, 19, 31, 68, 80, 104, 123, 134, 135
tabletop exercises, 104
tablets, 57
tacit knowledge, 49, 77
Tactical Action Officer Intelligent Tutoring System, TAO ITS, 99
tactical combat casualty care, 113
tactical decision-making, 21, 99
tactical planning, 111
theory of empowerment, 111
tourniquet, 22, 73, 113, 121
trade-offs, 15, 52–54, 135
Trainer for Advanced Life Support in Austere Regions, TALSAR, 22, 57–58
training
    adaptive, 91, 100, 103, 135
    didactic, 80
    error management, 23
    facilitator-led, 107
    flashcard, 55, 87, 122
    part-task, 70
    passive, 86
    perturbation, 45–47, 48
    scenario-based, 17, 55, 82
    scenario-based, definition, 15–16
    scenario-based, immersion, 19–21
    simulation-based, 30, 50, 133
    stand-alone, 15, 107, 118, 121, 124
    team, 27, 112, 118, 126
training environment, 18, 22, 69, 82, 91
training scars, 59
troubleshooting, 95
truck driving, 86

ultrasound, 57
usability, 134

video occlusion, 57
virtual colleague, 47, 123
Virtual Heroes Combat Medic, 65
Virtual Patient Immersive Trainer, VPIT, 71
virtual reality, 19, 134, 135
virtual tutor, 96
visual kinesthesis, 64
Vygotsky, Lev, 92–93

Ward, Paul, 88
Weatherwise, 55–56
word processors, 94

zone of available assistance, 99, 100
zone of capability, 94
zone of proximal adjustment, 100, 104
zone of proximal development, 92–93

For EU product safety concerns, contact us at Calle de José Abascal, 56–1°, 28003 Madrid, Spain or eugpsr@cambridge.org.

www.ingramcontent.com/pod-product-compliance
Ingram Content Group UK Ltd.
Pitfield, Milton Keynes, MK11 3LW, UK
UKHW020351140625
459647UK00020B/2396